GW00393976

Copyright Notice

Strolling Around The Hague by Irene Reid

ISBN: 9781799128786

Book Cover

Photo by Irene Reid

Enhanced by Prisma Photo Editor

Get Ready

The Mauritshuis and Prince William Gallery

If you like art you will definitely want to visit the Mauritshuis, to see "The Girl with the Pearl Earring" if nothing else.

Your ticket includes entrance to The Hague's second art gallery, the Prince William Gallery, thought by many to be a hidden gem.

You can pre-book your tickets here:

https://tickets.mauritshuis.nl/nl/tickets

The Peace Palace

The Peace Palace is well worth visiting but it's only open to the public on certain weekends.

If it's open when you are there you can buy tickets for a tour at the Visitors Centre, but be warned, they are limited in number. You could pre-book tickets, but they are only on sale a week or so in advance, so you do have to be very organised. The tours are in both Dutch and English.

Walk 4 gives you information on what you will see as you are guided around the Palace. Note, you cannot take photographs inside the Palace.

You can pre-book your tickets here:

https://www.vredespaleis.nl/visit/guided-tours/?lang=en

Binnenhof

The Binnenhof was the centre of Dutch government and is based in and around The Hague's old castle. You can visit if you buy a guided tour.

You can't actually buy the tickets in the Binnenhof itself. You can buy them at the Prodemos Visitor Centre at Hofweg 1 which lies just opposite the Binnenhof.

Alternatively you can pre-book tickets here:

http://english.prodemos.nl/English/Visitor-Centre/Guided-tours

Note, the tours are in Dutch but you will be given an English audio-guide. There are various combinations of tickets depending on what you want to see. So you could read about the Binnenhof on Page 22 to find out what appeals to you.

Once you have a time-slot arranged, you can easily fit it into Walk 1 as you will never be more than a short walk away.

Grote Kerk Tower

If you want to visit the tower of The Hague's biggest church, you can get tickets and book a time-slot here.

https://www.dehaagsetoren.nl/en/

Potted History

Holland and The Netherlands are often both used today to identify the same country, but in fact Holland is only the northern low-lying part of The Netherlands. It was ruled by The Counts of Holland until the sixteenth century.

The Hague actually grew up around a hunting lodge which Floris IV, the Count of Holland, had built next to a little pond in the thirteenth century.

His family liked the place so much that they later extended the lodge, and finally Count William II turned it into a castle in 1248. Parts of the castle grounds still exist, and are used today for official events and of course are explored by sightseers.

The village which grew up near the castle was named Hagga, which translates as hedge but is probably meant to be interpreted as Hunting Ground. It then became Graven Hage, (The Count's Hunting Ground) and the name GravenHage is still used today in traditional documents like marriage certificates. But to most people it's Den Haag, or The Hague.

From Counts to Kings

The "Count of Holland" title was eventually married away into the Royal families of Europe. The Hague was promoted to be the capital of Holland when the Dukes of Burgundy inherited the title.

The last Count of Holland was King Philip II of Spain. His father, Charles V, spoke Flemish and often visited Holland. Philip did not speak Flemish, didn't visit, imposed the Spanish Inquisition, and was universally loathed by the Dutch.

He was essentially kicked out by a ruling made in The Hague in 1581. The politicians decided that since he was such a bad king he wasn't fit for the job and he was stripped of his title. King Philip didn't take too kindly to that proposal and declared war – and that war lasted eighty years!

At the start of that war, the Dutch appointed William I of the House of Orange as their leader, and he led the campaign against Spain in many battles. He is the ancestor of today's Royal Family. The Dutch national anthem, the Wilhelmus, is a song in praise of William I – and he even has an asteroid, 12151 Oranje-Nassau, named after him.

At the end of the Eighty Year War, The Netherlands came into being incorporating Holland and other Flemish provinces. The House of Orange ruled The Netherlands from that time until the French under Napoleon marched in.

Napoleon

When Napoleon reached The Hague he demanded the keys to the city, perhaps not realising that a city without a city wall didn't actually have a key. The Hague depended on its surrounding canals for defense rather than a wall, and of course you can't lock a canal. Instead, the bridges over the canals were raised every night.

The city fathers thought fast and two impressive keys were rapidly cast and placed on a cushion to be presented to the Emperor to keep him happy – although they didn't open anything. Napoleon was pleased enough and later named The Hague as the Third City of the Kingdom.

When Napoleon was defeated, the Prince of Orange returned from exile and eventually became The Netherlands first King. His family has ruled ever since.

In the nineteenth century, Belgium and The Netherlands became one country for a short time, and the capital alternated between Amsterdam and Brussels.

Finally Belgium detached itself from The Netherlands, leaving Amsterdam as the capital, but oddly the seat of government was left in The Hague.

City of Peace

The Hague took on the role as the city of peace and justice. It is home to many international organisations which strive to keep the peace in the world. They built the Peace Palace in 1913 but war erupted in 1914 – perhaps not the best omen. The Peace Palace later housed the International Court of Justice.

The Hague was badly damaged during WWII. The RAF totally missed their target when bombing the occupying Germans, and sadly destroyed the historical centre.

After the war, The Hague became one of the biggest building sites in Europe and was reconstructed. Today only the very core of the old town survives.

The Maps

Each walk starts with an overview map, just to give you an idea of the route.

There are detailed map sections sprinkled through each walk to help you find your way.

If you need to check where you are at any point during a walk, always flip back to the previous map to find where you are.

To help you follow the maps, each map shows its start point. In addition numbered points have been placed on each map. The numbered points correspond to the numbered directions within the walks.

The Walks

Walk 1 (3.8 km)

This walk takes you around the oldest part of The Hague.

It starts in a square called Plein and includes a visit to the Mauritshuis to see the famous painting "Girl with a Pearl Earring" by Vermeer.

It then takes you west as far as the Grote Kerk, then south to the Grote Markt, before returning you to Plein.

Walk 2 (2.4 km)

This walk takes you along the lakeside and around one of The Hague's nicest canal areas. The return route passes various embassies, museums, and churches.

Walk 3 (2 km)

This walk takes you to the Noordeinde Palace and then north to the Mesdag Panorama Museum. You then return to the old town via some more interesting old streets.

Walk 4

This walk takes you to the Peace Palace.

Walk 1 – The Old City

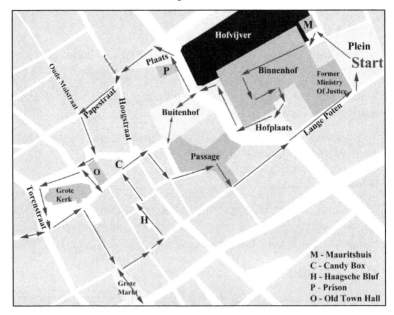

Walk 1 Overview

This walk starts in Plein, a large square in the old town.

It includes a visit to the Grote Kerk, so if you have pre-booked a slot to climb the tower, you can fit it in. You will never be more than a fifteen minute walk away from the church.

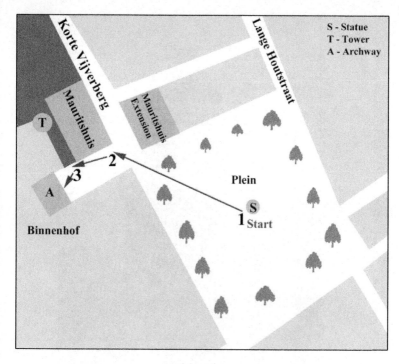

Map 1

Plein

This is now one of The Hague's main squares – in fact the name Plein means "Square". It's ringed by trees which provide visitors with some welcome shade in the summer. Outside the summer months you can browse around the antique book fair which fills the square.

Standing in the middle, you get an interesting contrast between the high rise buildings of the modern city looming above you on one side, and the surviving old town on the other.

The square was originally the kitchen garden of the castle where the Counts of Holland lived. At that time it was circled by canals – but they are all gone now. Later it was transformed into a beautiful ornamental garden, and it wasn't until the seventeenth century that it became a city square surrounded by handsome mansions and government buildings.

Until this century Plein was awash with parked cars. The Hague decided it was time to act, built an underground car park beneath the square, and once again Plein is a place for people to enjoy.

William I, Prince of Orange, stands in the middle of the square.

William I (William the Silent)

He used to point towards the old town and the castle, but he has been moved since then and now points to the skyscrapers towering over The Hague – perhaps asking "What on Earth?"

So where is Orange? It's actually in southern France in the Rhone valley, but it was given to one of William's ancestors as a reward for his part in the expulsion of the Moors from Europe. Of course Orange has long been part of France, but the family kept the title.

Like most royal families, the House of Orange insisted on using the same name over and over again, so it does get very confusing as to who is who. The House of Orange was obsessed by the name William and there are an awful lot of them.

This William was the eldest cousin of the reigning Prince of Orange who died without any children in the sixteenth century, leaving William to inherit the title.

He was brought up as a Lutheran (a protestant religion) but he decided to switch to Catholicism to ensure his inheritance. He always believed in the individual's freedom to choose a religion, but at the time the Netherlands was ruled by Catholic Spain, and choice of religion wasn't really an option. The Spanish inflicted their terrible Inquisition on the Dutch Protestants.

William was nicknamed William the Silent. Legend tells us that during a hunt he had a conversation with Philip II, and

13

listened carefully as the Spanish king declared his loathing of the Protestants and his plans for their removal. William stayed silent to hear the king's plans in full.

He then led the rebellion of the Dutch people which would eventually gain the Netherlands independence from Spain in 1648. In the process, he was declared an outlaw by the Spanish crown.

King Philip responded to the Dutch rebellion by offering a huge reward of 25,000 crowns for William's assassination. That tempted Frenchman Balthasar Gerard to track William down in Delft, and kill him by shooting him in the chest. His last words are reported to have been:

> My God, have pity on my soul;
> my God, have pity on these poor people.

He was the first head of state to be assassinated by a handgun.

Gérard was soon apprehended and brutally tortured to death. We are told that his right hand which fired the gun was burned off his arm with a red-hot iron. Then his skin was torn off, but while still alive he was disemboweled and finally decapitated. Gruesome!

Map 1.1 - Stand back to back with Prince William, and cross the square diagonally left to reach its left hand corner.

Just slightly to your left you will see a lovely building – this is the entrance to the Mauritshuis – it helpfully says Mauritshuis on the pediment of the building so it's easy to spot.

Mauritshuis

This is now the home of The Hague's main art collection.

It was originally a royal palace and later was used to lodge really important state visitors. The building was then bought by the Dutch Government to house the Royal Family's art collection, and it opened its doors to the public in 1822.

It was shut in 2012 for two years for renovation. Part of the renovation included the new underground entrance hall which you reach from a stairway in the front courtyard. The entrance hall gives access to the Mauritshuis itself which houses the permanent collection, and to another nearby building which is called The Extension and is used for temporary exhibitions.

If you visit the Mauritshuis, your ticket normally includes entrance to any temporary exhibition so it's worth looking to see what's on.

The Mauritshuis permanent collection contains many beautiful paintings. Here are some personal favourites to spot:

Girl with a Pearl Earring – Vermeer

This is where you will find the largest huddle of people, all probably trying to take a selfie with "The Girl".

Vermeer is famous for his paintings of Dutch women, but this is his masterpiece – it's been called "The Mona Lisa of Northern Europe". This seventeenth century painting has just resurfaced after a lengthy restoration, and you can now stand and look into the girl's eyes as she stares back at you.

'Girl with a Pearl Earring' was actually originally called 'Girl with a Turban' but was later renamed - Vermeer was fond of Turkish artefacts - hence the turban which would have been very exotic headgear for a simple Dutch girl.

The painting became very well known when a movie was made about it, starring Scarlett Johannsen as The Girl, and Colin Firth as Vermeer. The movie tells us of the strained relationship between the artist (who was married) and his model who was a servant.

The real model is not known for certain, but she is thought to have been Vermeer's daughter. There is a debate about the earing which if you look at it, is very large for a pearl. It's thought it might just be tin – but try to ignore that idea when you look at it.

Vermeer used lavish materials in his work. That vivid blue on the turban is from ultramarine, an extremely expensive pigment made from crushing Lapis Lazuli – if you see the movie you will see Vermeer and The Girl preparing the pigments. Lapis Lazuli was used by the Egyptians on their most expensive artifacts including Tutankhamun's Mask.

The painting was purchased for just a few guilders in 1881 as it was in very poor condition by then. It was later donated to the Mauritshuis with other paintings by the owner.

The Bull - Paulus Potter

Potter was famous for his animal paintings and this enormous scene is a good example. We see a farmer proudly gazing at his animals. The flies hovering around the bull really emphasize the kind of hot day being portrayed.

The artist took great care with the intricate details - spot the little frog sitting at the bull's feet and the lark in the sky. It's thought that the bull is an amalgam of the best features of several bulls of various ages – a kind of "best of" construction kit.

Paulus Potter's life is rather a sad story as he died young from tuberculosis.

The Anatomy Lesson of Dr. Nicolaes Tulp – Rembrandt

Doctor Tulp was the chief surgeon in Amsterdam as well as the Mayor. Rembrandt shows him giving an anatomy lesson to a group of eagerly watching surgeons. This was a major event each winter – when it was cold enough to prevent the corpse decaying too rapidly.

Amsterdam only allowed dissections of an executed criminal's body, so it was an event definitely not to be missed. The criminal in this case was Adriaan Adriaanszoon who was hung for armed robbery. Surgeons and ghoulish spectators attended these events and dressed as though going to theatre, as you can see.

When Rembrandt undertook this painting, Amsterdam's surgeons paid to be included in the painting, a kind of early advertising. The faces of the spectators seem genuinely engrossed in what they are seeing. Experts think Rembrandt used a medical textbook as his model of the arm being taken apart, rather than the real thing.

View of Delft – Vermeer

This painting is a favourite in The Netherlands and in 2011 it appeared on commemorative coins issued by the mint.

If you visit Delft while in The Netherlands, you can stand where this landscape would have been painted from - but of course the view is very different today. You can certainly still pick out the Nieuwe Kerk steeple which is the painting's centrepiece and seems to be bathed in sunshine – but most of the other details are long gone.

The way you hear it, the way you sing it - Jan Steen

This looks a very jovial painting - I think you can almost hear that wine glugging into that upheld glass. However Steen was also giving us a warning, both in the painting and its title. It's about adults setting a bad example to children, as in drinking and smoking. A further hint is the parrot in the corner which of course is a copycat, just like children.

It's thought that the chap giving his pipe to a child is actually Jan Steen himself.

The Messenger – Jan Verkolje

This painting tells the story of a messenger arriving with news which seems to be alarming to the recipient. I love it however because of the lady's gown in beautiful glowing satin.

The Garden of Eden, with the fall of men - Brueghel and Rubens

In this painting you see Adam and Eve living happily in Eden, but slithering down from the tree is the serpent about to throw a spanner in the works.

Brueghel painted the menagerie of animals surrounding Adam and Eve, which ranges from tigers to little guinea pigs just below Eve's feet. Rubens painted the nudes – which you might have guessed from the voluptuous style.

This is a joint effort from two great artists who were seemingly good friends. It's nice to imagine the two artists working at the same time, and perhaps chatting – however it seems they didn't work that way. Breughel would do his bit, leaving the appropriate spaces for Rubens to fill in. The painting was then delivered to Rubens' studio and the figures were inserted. Finally it would go back to Breughel to fill in the spaces around the figures and complete it.

Once you return to the entrance hall you can investigate any temporary exhibition on at the same time in The Extension.

Map 1.2 - When you exit the museum, leave by the main gate.

Turn right to approach the Binnenhof, the surviving buildings of the old castle.

As you reach the end of the Mauritshuis, look to your right to see the conical roof of Het Torentje.

Het Torentje

This little tower gets its first mention in historical documents in 1354, when it was a summer house connected by a drawbridge to the garden of the old castle. You will get a better view of the tower from the other side of the lake on Walk 2.

It is now the office of the prime minister; it was first used by Prime Minister Ruud Lubbers in 1982

Map 1.3 - Continue to approach The Binnenhof. The archway you see ahead of you is called the Mauritspoort.

Mauritspoort

Try to imagine what you see in front of you now, surrounded by a castle wall and canals. Most of the castle walls and canals are gone now, leaving us with just the surviving inner buildings of the castle (the Binnenhof), and this gateway.

The Mauritspoort was added to what remained of the old castle walls in the seventeenth century – it was to provide a very grand entrance for state visits. At that time the canal still ran round the castle, so this gateway was reached by a drawbridge.

Above the central gateway you can see The Hague's coat of arms guarded by two lions. If you look just below the two lions you can see the drawbridge pulley holes.

The two little side gates were added later in the nineteenth century for pedestrians. Now of course, we can all walk through the Mauritspoort and into the Binnenhof.

The Binnenhof

The Binnenhof is what is left of the complex of buildings which was once home to the Dutch rulers, and which was later where the Dutch parliament met.

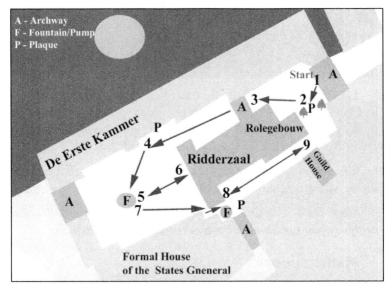

Map 2

Map 2.1 - Go through the archway and into the Binnenhof, the old castle grounds.

You will find yourself in a small square with three Linden trees on your left-hand side. You can see another gateway ahead of you.

Tennis Anyone!

Pause for a moment to find the granite plaque on the ground beneath the second tree.

It marks the spot of Holland's first tennis court and was gifted by the Orange Tennis Club. It translates as:

> On this place stood
> between about 1500 and 1650
> the country's first tennis court.
> "The Caetsbaan of the Princes of Orange"

Caetsen was an early version of tennis, and Kings Willem II and Willem III were both keen players.

Map 2.2 - Now approach the next archway which is called The Binnenpoort. The castle-like building with the tall turret, which you pass on the left as you do, is called the Rolgebouw.

Rolgebouw

The archaeologists have unearthed foundations and walls beneath the Rolgebouw which date from the thirteenth century. It's believed that they were part of the original hunting lodge built by Count Floris IV, as mentioned in the Potted History.

The Rolgebouw was built on top of those old foundations by Willem I, and it was there that the Counts of Holland resided as the castle complex slowly expanded and became the centre of the Count's realm.

Map 2.3 - Go through The Binnenport, the archway in front of you, to reach the main courtyard, the Binnenhof.

Walk straight ahead until you spot a large memorial plaque on your right. The building it sits on was the HofKapel.

Hofkapel

The High Chapel was built in the thirteenth century and was used for worship until the end of the nineteenth century. Sadly at that point it was converted into offices.

The plaque you see commemorates its previous role as a religious building, and it tells us that many of the graves of Holland's Counts and Countesses still lie in the cellar.

However it's thought that there is little chance of finding any complete skeletons down there. What was the floor of the HofKapel, has been dug up and disturbed more than once over the centuries. So even if bones were found, no-one would know who they belonged to.

One internee which the historians would love to find is Johan van Oldenbarnevelt.

Johan van Oldenbarnevelt

Oldenbarnevelt was a statesman and lawyer who passionately supported Dutch Independence from Spain.

Once that goal was achieved, he worked tirelessly with Prince Maurits of Orange to legislate for and to build the new country, The Netherlands.

Unfortunately as the years rolled by, Oldenbarnevelt and Prince Maurits became enemies, and as so often happens religion was the cause. Maurits demanded that The Netherlands follow the Catholic Church - Oldenbarnevelt wanted religious freedom for everyone.

Oldenbarnevelt was arrested and charged with treason, and after a very rigged trial he was executed. He was beheaded here in the Binnenhof and was buried in the Hofkapel.

It's said that his last words were to his executioner,

"Make it short, make it short".

The Dutch have tried very hard to locate his remains in the Hofkapel, but no luck so far.

Map 2.4 - Turn left and you will spot a golden fountain with gargoyles in the centre of the courtyard.

The fountain has undergone more than one restoration, so there is always the chance that when you visit, it will be under wraps or even in a workshop somewhere. So fingers crossed that you find it gleaming in the sunshine.

Fountain

The fountain was designed by Pierre Cuypers who also designed the Rijksmuseum in Amsterdam. It was exhibited at a huge Trade Exhibition in Amsterdam in 1883. Its aim was to showcase the artistry in blacksmithing – it's made of wrought iron.

Once the fair was over it was installed in the Binnenhof. To save precious water, it was only switched on during the summer months and special days such as Prince's Day.

At the top stands a golden statue of Count Willem II. Beneath the statue it states:

In memory of William II,
Roman King and Count of Holland,
supporter of city freedoms,
patron of the arts,
founder of the castles in The Hague and Haarlem

Map 2.5 – From the fountain you will see the very imposing twin-turreted building which sits in the centre of the courtyard. That is the Ridderzaal (The Knights Hall), so make your way towards it.

Ridderzaal

The Ridderzaal (Knights Hall) has survived from the 13th century when it was the banqueting hall of the castle.

The centuries took their toll on the building and it fell into a sorry state. The facade was restored in 1879, and the fountain which you just visited was a gift from 86 of The Hague's most prominent citizens, in appreciation of that much-needed restoration.

If you take the tour round the Binnenhof you will see inside the Ridderzaal.

Inside the Ridderzaal

The roof collapsed in the eighteenth century but was beautifully restored. It is made from Irish oak and resembles an upturned ship and it is really worth seeing.

Look up at the supporting columns to see some small heads peering down at you. Those were put there to remind people gathered below, that a higher power was watching, and that the truth must be told.

Above the fireplace are the first lines of the Dutch constitution.

The hall also boasts a lovely Rose window sporting the coats of arms of the noble families of Holland. You can see the rose window from the courtyard above the main door, but of course you need to be inside to see the colourful stained glass.

If you visit the cellar you will see some of the tombstones which have been rescued from the old Hofkapel.

Kings Speech

The Ridderzaal is where the King is driven to in his Golden Carriage once a year, to give his speech and to open parliament. The King's throne in the hall is decorated with a crown and the Dutch Coat of Arms.

After the King's speech, the Finance Minister opens his briefcase and reads the budget. The tradition of using a briefcase is very similar to that used by the British Chancellor of the

Exchequer on budget day, and started in 1947. The original briefcase lasted until 1964 by which time it was showing definite wear and tear. The Finance Minister now uses one given as a gift by the Government Printing Office.

Map 2.6 - Return to the fountain and turn to face the Ridderzaal once more.

The Houses

The Dutch government has two parliamentary bodies, the Upper House and the Lower House – just like the House of Lords and the House of Commons in the UK.

The Upper House receives bills from the Lower House and decides if they should be made law immediately or if more discussion is required.

De Erste Kammer

The building running along your left hand-side is De Erste Kammer, the political heart of the Netherlands for centuries. It is where the Upper House of the Dutch government sits.

It has a much more attractive facade which you will see later on the walk.

Inside De Erste Kammer

The ceiling is decorated with people from the trading nations of The Netherlands – all keeping an eye on what The Netherlands is up to.

You can see representatives of Poland, Russia, Turkey, Mexico, France, Italy, Germany, and the Persians – see how many you can identify.

At one time the inner walls were covered in glorious tapestries, but they were pinched during the Napoleon era, shipped to Paris, and never seen again. The tapestry you see now was made in Grenoble by computer aided design as part of the restoration.

There is a very large painting of King William II – he gets pride of place because it was under his reign in 1848, that the constitution was amended. It gave the power to elect the government to the people rather than the monarchy.

Formal House of the States General

Now look to the building on your right. The Lower House used to sit in the ballroom which was in this building, but the politicians have been moved into a more modern building which you will see shortly.

Map 2.7 – Face the Ridderzaal again and go down its right-hand side. You will reach another archway on your right, and on the wall beside the archway is a plaque.

Das Englandspiel

The plaque was put up in memorial to those who died during Das Englandspiel, or The England Game.

During WWII the British dropped agents into the Netherlands to aid the Dutch resistance; however the Germans discovered the landing sites and apprehended the first arrivals. The Germans forced the captured agents to respond to the British over radio, in order to gain vital information and managed to intercept further agent drops.

The captured agents tried to alert London to the problem by omitting the vital security codes they should have used in the transmissions, but not only did London not take action on the missing codes, on one occasion they actually radioed back to tell the operator to use them – which of course alerted the Germans to the omission. A complete intelligence disaster!

It is said that one British operator was suspicious and ended his transmission with HH, short for Heil Hitler – and the agent in Holland responded back immediately with HH. You can almost envisage the arm salute! The British operator alerted his superiors to his suspicions, but they ignored the information completely.

Finally two Dutch agents, code-named Sprout and Chive, managed to escape back to the UK and alerted intelligence of the problem. The Germans realised their deception was over and sent a mocking final message to British Intelligence just before D-Day:

> "We understand that you have been trying for some time to do business in Holland without our assistance. We regret this the more since we have acted for so long as your sole representatives in this country, to our mutual satisfaction. Should you be thinking of paying us a visit on the Continent, we shall give your emissaries the same attention as we have hitherto."

In all about fifty allied agents lost their lives during this campaign – you don't see that incident portrayed in the any of the many war movies.

Water Pump

There is a large impressive water pump opposite the plaque. You will see a few more pumps as you explore The Hague – there were over seventy in the city at one time.

Map 2.8 - Before you go through the archway, walk on a little further into the Binnenhof.

Further down on your right hand side, you will find a little building which was the Guild House.

It was the guild house of the goldsmiths; one of The Hague's richest which is probably why it stands here in the Binnenhof. It was here that the work produced by the various smiths was inspected for quality.

The building has the following words written above the door in colourful lettering:

t 'Goutsmits Keur Huys

Now if you could speak Dutch you would spot the spelling mistake immediately. Apparently it should read:

't Goutsmits Keur Huys

The apostrophe is in the wrong place.

Map 2.9 - Return to the Englandspiel plaque.

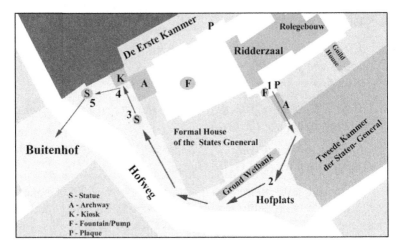

Map 3

Map 3.1 - Go through the archway next to the Englandspiel plaque.

You will find yourself at the side of the new Parliament Building. Walk to the front of the semi-circular Parliament Building and onto the triangular square called Hofplaats.

Tweede Kamer der Staten-Generaal

The parliament building is called the Tweede Kamer der Staten-Generaal building, and is where the Lower House now sits.

As mentioned, the Lower House used to sit in the ballroom of the Binnenhof. However it was too small for the number of participants and the old public galleries shuddered under the weight of the viewers. So a new building was planned.

Since the new parliament building was to sit next to the Binnenhof, a very conscious decision was taken to try to make it "fit" in – you can decide yourself if they succeeded.

The new building uses a great deal of very modern glass – the idea was that government was transparent with no secrets, and

32

that the politicians should always be looking out to the real world – both nice ideas but not ones which are always achieved.

The second material used was granite – solid and enduring and again to illustrate what the Dutch parliament was to embody.

Now, face away from the Tweede Kamer, and running along the right of Hofplaats you will see the GrondWetBank.

GrondWetBank

This is a long granite bench on which is engraved the First article of the constitution. It translates as:

> All persons in the Netherlands, in similar cases should be treated alike.
> Discrimination on the grounds of religion, belief, political opinion, race, gender or any other grounds whatsoever shall not be permitted.

Map 3.2 - Walk the length of the bench to reach the main road which is called Hofweg.

Turn right to walk along the side of the Binnenhof. You will reach a very modern statue of Prime Minister Willem Drees

Willem Drees Statue

He was the politician who fought to give the elderly an automatic state pension, so he is one of the good guys – or maybe he had a vested interest as he lived to the ripe old age of 102!

Notice the large red circle on the ground beside him – a symbol of socialism.

Map 3.3 - A little further on you will see an archway on your right which gives access back into the Binnenhof. A few more steps will bring you to a popular Herring stall.

Dutch Herring

Herring is a very popular street-food in The Netherlands and this little kiosk is a good place to try it.

It comes with onions and pickles. If you want you can request it in a sandwich, it's called a broodje haring.

Map 3.4 – A few steps to the left will bring you to a statue of King William II on his horse.

King William II

He was a grandson of William the Silent and he is shown here in full uniform on his horse. He fought at Waterloo where he was injured by musket shot; he was seen as a great hero by his people.

The base of this monument used to hold a lead casket which contained two biographies of the king. An attempt was made to restore the casket in 1993, but it was found that the rain over the years had damaged it so badly that it could not be repaired.

The statue is a copy, the original is in Luxembourg. It is beautifully lit up at night, so if you are in the area in the evening, try to pass by.

Map 3.5 - Cross the busy road carefully to reach another square, it is called Buitenhof.

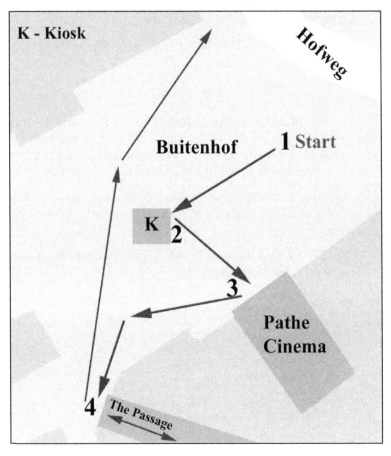

Map 4

Buitenhof

This square was originally a private enclosure attached to the Binnenhof. It was bordered by the Prison, the Stables, and various other buildings.

It wasn't until the nineteenth century that access to it was opened up. New roads were built, including the busy Hofweg which you have just crossed.

Map 4.1 - Make your way to the odd little kiosk in the centre of the square

Berlage Kiosk

This is a national monument!

The original old flowers and magazine stall which once stood here was replaced in the thirties by this modern concrete construction. It was designed by Berlage, one of The Netherlands best known architects. Remember that name as you will come across it again.

At the time of writing the kiosk has been turned into a café, so you could sip a drink while you decide if you like it.

Map 4.2 - Stand by the kiosk, with the Binnenhof and the Hofweg behind you.

On your left-hand side at number 20 is the Pathé cinema. Make your way towards it.

Pathé Cinema

It has some beautiful art nouveau balconies and stonework. It has been restored both inside and outside, and so far has remained a cinema. It has another nice café if needed.

Map 4.3 - Face the Pathé building.

Turn right and walk to the corner of the square, where you will find the entrance to The Passage.

The Passage

This is the country's first covered shopping arcade. The entrance is decorated with columns and two cast iron statues of agriculture and industry. The dates at the top, 1882-1885, are the years of construction.

Right at the top of the entrance you can spot a stork. The Hague coat of arms boasts a stork, and you will see storks on many of the old buildings in The Hague.

In medieval times The Hague was surrounded by lakes, marshes and meadows. It was a paradise for wildlife and storks flocked there. They became almost tame and walked freely around The Hague – some were even trained to clean up the fish market of debris – although it probably didn't take too much training.

Take a walk inside The Passage and try to imagine The Hague's wealthy residents doing the same in the nineteenth century.

The Passage stretches quite a way, so explore as far as you like and then return to the entrance on Buitenhof.

Note; there is no need to walk beyond the domed crossroads in the Passage, as you will enter The Passage again later in this walk.

Map 4.4 – Once back outside The Passage, turn right to return to the square. Cross it diagonally to reach the busy Hofweg once more.

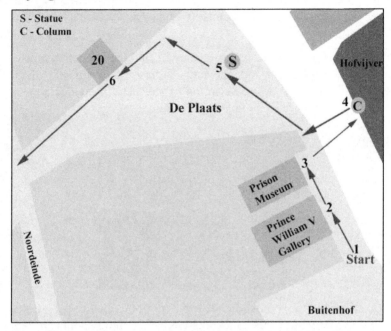

Map 5

Map 5.1 – Face the little lake and turn left to walk along the Hofweg.

You will soon reach the Prince William V Gallery on your left.

If you don't intend to visit, continue from "To the Prison" on page 42.

Prince William V Gallery

This pretty art gallery was built by yet another William, Prince William V, in the eighteenth century to show off his art collection. The whole collection was pinched by the French and installed in Paris when they ruled The Netherlands, but it was later returned.

The collection was at one point housed in the Mauritshuis, but The Gallery has been restored and has taken back some of the original collection.

If you go in to this gallery, you will find the collection housed in one small room and one long gallery. Pick up one of the provided guides for a description of any painting which appeals to you. Here are some favourites to find:

Cows – Paulus Potter

You may have already seen the enormous painting by Potter in the Mauritshuis. He does seem to have a thing about cattle!

Here is a smaller painting with cows down at the river. What is interesting about this one is the reflection of the cows in the river, and the herdsmen skinny dipping in the summer sun.

The Toothpuller – Jan Steen

This is the sort of painting that makes you thankful you live in today's modern world. Dentistry was a fearful business.

You have to laugh at the expression on the young boy to the left of the victim – he is clearly enjoying the show.

Hunting Party near the Hofvijver in The Hague

This painting is strategically placed near a window where you can see the viewpoint used by the artist. You should recognise the viewpoint, as you have just left it. The scene does look more idyllic than the modern reality.

Portrait of a Young Woman – Rubens

This is a portrait of Ruben's young wife Hélène Fourment–
she was just 16 and he was 53 – but that wasn't very unusual in
those days. He loved her dearly and painted her many times,
both as a portrait like this one, and as a model in many other
works.

You can also compare it with his first wife, Isabella Brandt,
as her portrait is also in this gallery.

To the Prison

*Map 5.2 - On leaving the Gallery, turn left. The next
building is the old Prison.*

If you decide to visit the prison, you will see the various
rooms on a guided tour. You will be given an audio guide to
use, as the tours are officially in Dutch. However if you are
lucky your guide will be happy to translate as he goes along.

You will be led upstairs, downstairs, and through the various
rooms. Your guide (audio or tour) will explain the purpose of
each room, the horrors of interrogation, and the power of money
to make even prison life a bit more bearable. The tour takes
about half an hour and is quite interesting

If you don't intend to visit, continue from "To the Lake" on page 45.

Inside the Prison

The prison building was originally part of the outer gateway of the castle, which was called Gevangenpoort. It made a handy prison when one was needed in the fifteenth century.

Initially it only housed the many unfortunates who were awaiting trial.

It was not unusual to be incarcerated for months in its cold dark cells, but that was not deemed punishment, merely an inconvenience.

Punishment when handed out was brutal, from flogging to execution. Thieves and beggars ran the risk of being branded or having fingers and hands cut off. Spies would risk having their eyes gouged out.

Later they added more cells and the prison was used to hold convicted criminals – they even added a Women's Room. Next a courtroom was built and the judge would either pass sentence, or perhaps send the prisoner to undergo "interrogation", which meant torture until the judge got the answer he wanted.

Like many prisons in Northern Europe at the time, if you had money life wasn't quite so bad. Wealthy inmates were held in The Knights Chamber, The Ridderkamer, which was a luxury cell complete with bed and fireplace.

The prison was finally closed in the nineteenth century and was at first used by the military to stash their weapons in. However it was decided to reclaim the building as a monument in 1883, to let the people peep into the horrors of the past.

It was threatened with demolition in the twentieth century to widen the Hofweg. However it was saved by filling in a bit of the little lake opposite in order to widen the Hofweg on that side instead.

The prison had some colourful inmates over the years:

Catherine de Chasseur

Catherine de Chasseur was an innkeeper's daughter who managed to marry Gerrit van Assendelft, the son and heir of a very powerful family – a very advantageous marriage on her part.

His family was not amused, and it was not long before Gerrit tried to abandon Catherine. However they were legally married and he was ordered by the court to support her. This he did from a distance via an annuity and thereafter ignored her.

Catherine wanted more than that and took the decision to take up forgery and mint her own coins. She was caught and condemned to burn at the stake in public. Her horrified Assendelft in-laws pulled strings and instead she was executed behind closed doors, to save them the humiliation of a member of the family being executed in public.

Catherine was tied to a rack, a funnel was put in her mouth and water was poured into it until she drowned – a truly horrible way to die. No-one knows where she was buried.

Hendrik Jut

Another famous inmate was Hendrik Jut. He murdered a young woman and was sentenced to life imprisonment, as the death penalty had just been abolished. The public were outraged and wanted blood, so the authorities moved Jut out of The Hague's prison to Leeuwarden prison to keep him safe.

An enterprising fairground stall holder had an inspiration. He built a contraption called Kop van Jut, which let the public smash a sledgehammer onto a gauge hard enough to ring a bell, and imagine it was Jut's head. It was a great success and you can still see its descendants in fairgrounds today.

To the Lake

Map 5.3 - From the Prison gate, carefully cross the busy road and have a look at the Hofvijver.

Hofvijver

Before the Hunting Lodge was built for Count Floris IV, a little waterway known as the Haagse Beek (The Hague Brook) ran along here and formed the little lake.

Once the castle was built, the brook was used to fill the moat around the castle and the lake was enlarged. The lake was named the Hofvijver.

The Haagse Beek is still there but it runs underground, from the Peace Palace (which you can visit on another walk), to here at the Hofvijver.

Canals were also dug to send water from the Haagse Beek around The Hague, where it was used first as a source of water and later as a sewer. Thankfully those polluted canals were filled and proper sewers were built in the nineteenth century.

The Hofvijver surrounds a little island which is quite a recent addition having been built about three hundred years ago. It's off-limits, but is a popular place during demonstrations, as the locals emphasize their point by invading the island and draping the trees with banners.

Memorial column

You will see a memorial column on the bridge. It commemorates the houses which once lined this side of the Hofvijer but which were demolished in 1923 to let the cars whizz along.

The memorial was designed by Berlage, the same architect of the little kiosk you saw earlier on Buitenhof. At the top is the stork, The Hague's favourite symbol, and underneath it marks the year of the demolition.

Map 5.4 - Now re-cross Hofweg carefully.

Turn right to reach a triangular square which is called Plaats and another statue.

Plaats

This square was the forecourt of the castle. Later in the Middle Ages it became a tournament field.

Green Zoodje

The Green Zoodje was The Hague's scaffold where executions took place. It used to stand just outside the Prison Gate on this square.

When the sentence was death the condemned met their fate on this scaffold, which got its name because it was floored with grass. Grass was much more efficient in soaking up all the blood than a wooden floor.

The court would announce an upcoming execution and encourage the townspeople to come to view the proceedings. The public would arrive out of morbid curiosity, which was exactly what the court wanted – the gruesome spectacle emphasized the power of the law.

The stone scaffold was eventually removed in the eighteenth century after complaints from wealthy neighbours. Instead whenever an execution was needed, a temporary wooden scaffold was put up for the job.

Johan de Witt

The statue is of Johan de Witt.

He was a merchant who picked up the reins of power when William II Prince of Orange died, leaving the infant William III as his heir.

Johan, a staunch Republican, took command and led the country through the Dutch Golden Age as William III grew up. His brother Cornelius was a successful naval commander who

47

led naval attacks against England and defended Holland's shores from power hungry neighbouring countries. However the brothers' luck ran out as the country's fortunes started to decline and William III turned against the De Witts.

Cornelius was arrested for treason against the House of Orange, which most historians believe was a trumped up charge to get rid of him. His bother went to the prison on the evening Cornelius was released, but the brothers were ambushed by a mob organised by their political opponents and stabbed to death.

The mob hung them upside down on the Green Zoodie, and cut off various bits of their bodies which were then either sold as souvenirs or apparently cooked and eaten. If you ever read "The Black Tulip" by Alexander Dumas you will read all about it. The whole incident paints modern politics in a much rosier light.

The statue you see shows Johan pointing to the spot where he and his brother were murdered by the mob.

Aleid van Poelgeest

If you stand face to face with Johan and look down just to the left of the statue, you should see a stone which commemorates another political murder. However, it seems the stone was "accidently" dug up and removed during some works on the square. So it may or may not have been restored when you visit.

Aleid van Poelgeest was the beautiful young mistress of Albert, Count of Holland, in the fourteenth century. She was attacked and murdered on this spot by the political enemies of the Count.

If you visit the Hague Historical Museum on Walk 2, you will have the chance to see some depictions of her untimely end.

Map 5.5 - Stand back to back with Johan and walk along the right-hand side of the square to reach number 20.

20 Plaats

This building has been restored to its original Art Nouveau decoration, so look up to see the colourful mosaics and intricate stonework. Above the door you can spot another stork.

The building was originally owned by Goupil and Cie, an art dealership. Vincent Van Gogh worked here for some time when he was just 16, and in his letters to his brother he wrote how much he liked living in The Hague.

This building was later bought by hatter J. van Dooren & Co, and his name still runs across the building.

Map 5.6 - Continue along the side of Plaats to reach its narrowest point and a T-junction.

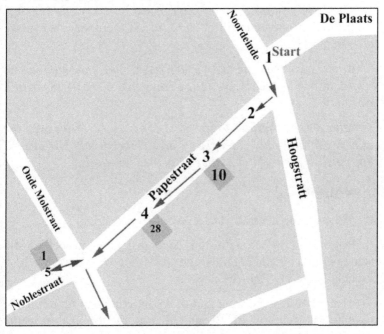

Map 6

Map 6.1 - Turn left into Noordeinde, and then almost immediately turn right into Papestraat.

49

Papestraat is one of the oldest streets in The Hague.

Map 6.2 - Walk along to find number 10 on your left-hand side.

10 Papestraat

This is an interesting Art Deco building with its multi-coloured bricks forming the pattern of the upper floors. Don't miss spotting the lovey side columns decorated with what look like thistles.

Map 6.3 – Continue to reach number 28 – also on your left.

28 Papestraat

This lovely old building was designed by JW Bosboom, and if you look at the bottom left hand side of the door you can see his signature.

It has an ornate wooden façade and if you look up you can see the art-deco decoration with a rising sun dated 1898 when it was built.

Map 6.4 - Continue to the next crossroads. Walk over the crossroads and take a few steps into Nobelstraat. The second building on the right at number 1 is the Nobelhuis.

Nobelhuis

The building helpfully has its name over the door.

It's thought to be one of the oldest residential properties still standing in The Hague, although to be honest it does not look especially elderly from the outside.

That's because the front part of the building was rebuilt in the seventeenth century, but behind that is the original fifteenth century building.

In the attic is one of The Hague's secret chapels. It was installed in 1627 and was used until a bigger church opened nearby in 1692.

It's a private residence so you can't visit unfortunately.

Map 6.5 - Return to the crossroads and turn right down Oude Molstraat.

Oude Molstraat

In the middle ages this was just a track running through the dunes which filled this area. When people began to build along it, they followed the original path as it wiggled its way through The Hague.

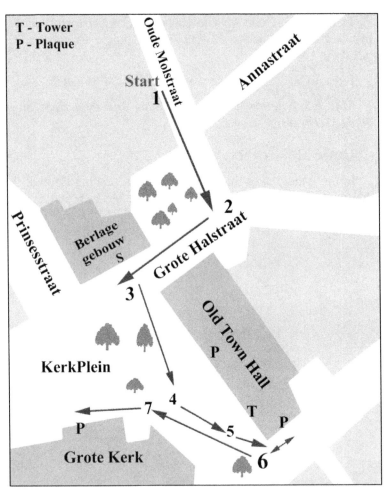

T - Tower
P - Plaque

Oude Molstraat

Annastraat

Start
1

2

Berlage gebouw S

Prinsesstraat

Grote Halstraat

3

Old Town Hall

KerkPlein

P

4

7

T

P

5

P

Grote Kerk

6

Map 7

Map 7.1 – Pass Annastraat on your left, and then walk into a little square which is usually filled with café tables.

A few more steps will bring you to a T-junction with Grote Halstraat where you can see tram-lines.

Map 7.2 - Turn right and you will see the tower of the Grote Kerk (Big Church) ahead of you.

Walk towards it but pause at the first building on your right.

Berlage Gebouw

It is called the Berlage Gebouw after Berlage (Kiosk man) who was the architect.

It was built for the De Nederlanden 1845 insurance company. The head of that company was a friend and admirer of Berlage, so commissioned him to design the new company offices.

Its façade is full of interesting details.

Above the door you can see the coat of arms of De Nederlanden 1845. The door is flanked by a horse's head and a bull's head – they represent farming.

There are also sixteen shields along the façade, celebrating the countries and cities which the company did business with. They are all named for easy identification:

Antwerp, Chile, Havana, Bombay, Calcutta, Transvaal, Norway, West India, East India, Denmark, Sweden, Marseille, Bremen, Hamburg, Paris and Bordeaux.

There is also a statue of Death looming over you which is a bit macabre, until you remember that it's an insurance company. There are three other statues you could see if you walked around the building, Fire, Home, and Family – all things any insurance company would be interested in selling insurance for.

Map 7.3 – Turn to face the church and then walk into Kerkplein, the square which surrounds the Church.

The Old Town Hall runs down the side of the square on your left. Walk over to get a good look at it.

Old Town Hall

You will see that the building has a split personality.

The larger left-hand part with its many windows is quite sedate. Above the central part is a stork and it is flanked by Justice and Prudence.

Beneath them you can read the wise words:

"Felix quem faciunt aliena pericula cautum"
or
"Wise men learn by other's errors, fools by their own"

Map 7.4 – A few steps further along will bring you to a much older and prettier part of the Town Hall.

It is much more colourful and exuberant. It was built in the sixteenth century on the foundations of the original village hall.

It has an ornate tower and the red shutters are very eye-catching. The tower contains two bells which are only rung at 12:30 and 13:30 – so check your watch to see if it's worth hanging around.

Map 7.5 – Keep the Town Hall on your left and walk round the corner. Here you see the most colourful side of the Town Hall. Across the top of the façade you can read:

Ne Jupiter Quedem Omnibus
or
Even Jupiter can't please everyone

which is a very pragmatic thought for a town council.

The Old Town Hall is nowadays used mainly for weddings, so if you are lucky you might see a bride arriving or departing.

Map 7.6 - Backtrack into Kerkplein again. The church will now be on your left-hand side.

Grote Kerk

The church is dedicated to St James and is one of the oldest in The Hague; there has been a church on this spot since the thirteenth century.

The Dead

The church square was investigated by archaeologists in 2005, as the church was having new toilets installed and it was too good an opportunity to miss.

They discovered that the area around the church was a seventeenth century cemetery and several complete skeletons were unearthed.

A year later the church floor was replaced, so again the archaeologists turned up with their shovels and investigated what was under there. It was only in 1830 that burials had to take place outside the church for hygiene reasons. Before that date, the very rich were interred under the church floor, so it was not a great surprise when they found graves. The term "filthy rich" comes from the stench the churchgoers had to endure whenever someone with enough fortune was buried inside the church.

The archaeologists then found something they did not expect, a basement full of thousands of bones and skulls, probably the townspeople who were not rich enough to get a grave in the main church floor.

Map 7.7 – Keep the church on you left and walk along its longer side. About half-way along spot a large plaque on the wall by one of the doors.

Prinses Irene Brigade

The plaque commemorates the Prinses Irene Brigade.

The Dutch troops who managed to escape to Great Britain in 1940 formed a brigade to fight for their homeland. The Brigade was named after Princess Irene who was born in 1939, the year World War II started.

They served in India and Surinam and were later brought back to Europe to join in its liberation. The plaque commemorates their part in the liberation of The Hague on May 8th 1945.

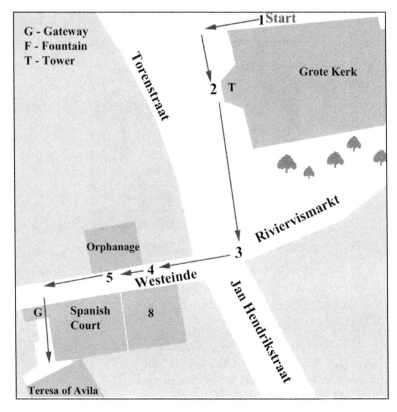

Map 8

Map 8.1 – Continue around the church and you will reach the church tower.

Note, this is where you will enter the tower if you plan to climb it.

The Tower

The church itself faces onto Torenstraat (Tower Street), which is of course named after the church's high six-sided bell tower. It is 92.5 metres high, and it's one of the tallest in the Netherlands.

58

At the top is a weather vane in the shape of - a stork!

The church tower was hit by lightning in 1539 and was more or less destroyed – the bells smashed to the ground. They rebuilt the tower a few years later, and raised the money by running a lottery for funds. Lightning hit again in 1702, but this time a young hero raced upstairs in his nightshirt and beat the flames out.

The Bells

The bells have their own dramatic survival story. There were originally five major bells, Jacob, Jhezus, Salvator, Maria, and Wege Waert. Maria was melted down and turned into a cannon in the sixteenth century.

The bell tower fell silent during WWII, and the Germans decided to melt the surviving bells. They ignored Wege Waert as it was thought too small to be worth the effort. Jhesus was too big to get out the church – although it makes you wonder how they got it in there. Jacob was taken by ship to Germany but the ship sank, and Jacob was fished out again after the war. Salvator did get to Germany but they didn't melt it, instead it was hung in Hamburg and also recovered after the war.

After the war a carillon was installed and the bells still ring today, especially at New Year – the bells peal out for five minutes at midnight.

If you don't want to visit the Grote Kerk, continue this walk from "Leave the Church" on Page 61.

If you don't want to visit the Grote Kerk, continue this walk from "Leave the Church" on Page 61.

Note, The Grote Kerk is used a lot for corporate events these days. It's only open to the public at the weekend and even then, only if nothing else is on. So you may find it closed. Hopefully you will be in luck and can visit.

Inside the Grote Kerk

If you do manage to get inside you will find it full of light, as the walls, roof, and column are all white. As you look round you might be surprised at the emptiness – the church had twelve beautiful chapels in the sixteenth century, but they were demolished one by one, leaving just what you see now.

On either side of the church are 34 panels bearing the shields and names of the Knights of the Golden Fleece.

The Order of the Golden Fleece

The Order of the Golden Fleece was dreamt up by the Duke of Burgundy in the fifteenth century – he owned The Hague at the time. His idea was to create a principled body of knights who would make judgment and give advice on disputes over the lands of his territories. The knights met in The Hague in 1456 and held court in both the Knights Hall and the Great Church. The coats of arms you see are those who attended. The Order expanded until the seventeenth century, and it still exists today and has powerful members - King Philip of Belgium became a Knight in 2008.

The Pulpit

Admire the wonderfully carved oak pulpit with its five panels depicting Mathew, Mark, Luke, John, and John the Baptist. The upper panel against the pillar shows us Moses and his ten commandments.

Walk towards where you would expect to find the altar.

Admiral Jacob van Wassenaer Obdam

Instead there is a very striking tomb in memory of Admiral Jacob van Wassenaer Obdam. Fame stands behind the Admiral blowing her trumpet, and the admiral is in full armour.

He was a commander during the second war against the English in the seventeenth century. His fleet attacked the English fleet at the battle of Lowestoft, but they were out-maneuvered and it turned into the worst naval defeat the Dutch had ever suffered. The flagship exploded and Obdam's body was lost at sea and never recovered – only five sailors survived from that ship.

Walk around to the rear of the admiral. One of the church's treasures is a beautiful stained-glass window given by the Holy Roman Emperor Charles V in 1539. You can see the Emperor kneeling in prayer before the Virgin Mary

Christiaan Huygens

One of The Hague's most famous sons was Christiaan Huygens. He was respected in many fields but he is best known as an astronomer. He discovered Saturn's rings and its moon Titan, the second largest moon in the Solar System – beaten only by Jupiter's Ganymede. When the European Space Agency launched a probe to Titan, of course they called it Huygens. He is buried in this church.

The Assendelft Chapel

One chapel which did survive is the Assendelft chapel, which contains the alabaster tomb of Gerrit van Assendelft and his wife Beatrix from the fifteenth century. They are lying as though sleeping.

Members of the Assendelft family were buried in this chapel until the mid-sixteenth century. Nowadays it's used for weddings and classical music concerts.

Exit the church.

Leave the Church

Map 8.2 – Return to base of the Church Tower. Face away from the tower door and turn left to approach a crossroads.

Map 8.3 – Once at the crossroads turn right into Westeinde and walk along to number 8 on your left.

Distillery

This building has the words

Firma J. Zondag – Wijnhandel – Distilleerderij

written in green and yellow tiles which run along above the doors and windows.

It was of course a distillery, which was owned and run by the Zondag family. They had their own secret recipes for lemon gin and blackcurrant gin.

Map 8.4 - Continue along Westeide to reach a house on your right-hand side which is set back from the road.

Orphanage

An orphanage has stood here since the sixteenth century. It was rebuilt a few times and later expanded to have a school.

Originally the orphanage took in all orphaned children, but later only the cleverest children went here, and the rest were sent to less salubrious accommodation.

This building was the orphanage's last incarnation but it is now private apartments. The inscription above the door says:

Ubi amicitia ibi bene

Where there is friendship, life is good

Map 8.5 – A few more steps will bring you to number 12 on your left-hand side. It has a very grand gateway.

Spanish Court

The building you have just passed on your left is the Spanish Court.

If you remember the story of Catherine de Chasseur from your visit to the Prison, you will be interested to know that she is supposed to haunt this building because this is where her home stood. There have been many reported sightings.

The Spanish Court itself is not open to the public, but you can sometimes enter the gate in front of you, which is topped by two lions guarding the Spanish coat of arms. If it's open, go through to reach St Teresia of Avila.

St Teresia of Avila

The original church on this spot was built for the Spanish Catholics associated with the Spanish Court and was officially off-limits to The Hague's catholic citizens, but that rule was routinely ignored.

Eventually the church was deemed too small for the number of worshipers and was replaced by the lovely church you see in front of you. It was completed in 1841 as is stated on the facade – which is seven years before the constitution gave religious freedom to everyone, but clearly attitudes were relaxing.

Unfortunately the church is often closed but if you are lucky, do go in as it's a beautifully bright church and worth a visit.

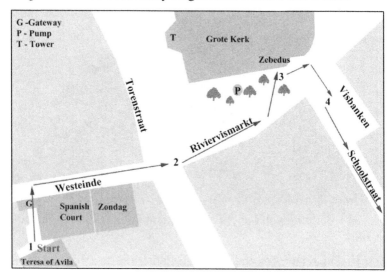

Map 9

Map 9.1 – Return through the gateway, and then turn right to backtrack along Westeinde.

Map9 .2 - When you reach the crossroads once more, continue straight ahead along Riviervismarkt. The Grote Kerk will be on you left-hand side. Pause when you approach the end of the church.

Zebedeus

If you would like a refreshment or a meal in an interesting location, you could visit Zebedeus on your left. It is a restaurant in one of the church outbuildings – it was the church vestry in the early twentieth century.

City Pump and Tree

Just outside the restaurant you will see another of the old city water pumps and an impressive old London Plane tree.

The tree is listed as one of The Hagues "Monumental Trees" so it is carefully looked after.

Map 9.3 – Keep the church on your left and walk a little further along following the tramlines. Take the next right into a little square called Visbanken.

Visbanken

This was a fish market from the sixteenth century. It was filled with purpose-built stalls which were rented to the fishmongers who used them to display their wares.

It was here that storks were kept and trained to clean up the fishy debris. Eventually the storks were relocated to the Hofijver and the square was cleaned using chemical cleaning products instead.

The fish market was last used in 1938, and after the war the stalls were used by booksellers for a while. The old stalls were swept away in 1970.

Map 9.4 - Leave the square by Schoolstraat which you will find on the far right corner.

It's pretty obvious that Schoolstraat is named after a school. Although the street name has survived, the school itself has long gone.

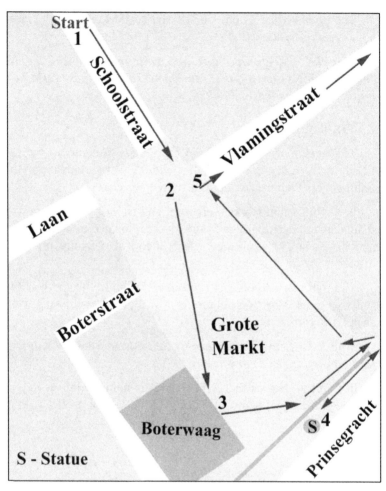

Map 10

Map 10.1 - You will walk into a large square called Grote Markt.

Grote Markt

This square now hosts an array of inns, and one worth a look is the Boterwaag.

Map 10.2 - Cross the square diagonally right to reach it.

The Boterwaag

This is where butter was weighed for market.

The left-half of this building is beautiful and designed and decorated by the city architect who was also the leader of the Guild of St. Luke. That guild had painters, sculptors, and many other types of artists in its ranks. Later the painters broke rank and formed a separate brotherhood and they met upstairs in this building. Note the pretty stork above the door.

The right half of the building was built as an extension in the seventeenth century and the business of weighing butter moved there.

The weighing house is now a very popular café and is worth a visit. Inside you can admire the high vaulted brick ceiling and the old weighing scale used to weigh the butter – it sits on the left hand side of the hall as you enter.

Map 10.3 - Once back outside, stand with Boterwag behind you.

Look diagonally right to spot the entrance to the Tram Station.

A 14th Century Convent in the Tram Station

In the fourteenth century a convent stood where the Grote Markt stands – but it's all gone now. However, when the tramway system was being built a tunnel was needed, and the diggers discovered all sorts of relics from the convent.

Some of them have been incorporated into the tram station platform wall, which is a nice touch.

Walk around the fence which sits above the tram station entrance. You will find Haagse Harry.

Haagse Harry

Harry is a Dutch comic character who first appeared in 1991. He is a gentle parody of the people of The Hague who have taken him to their hearts.

He is noisy, rude, and swears a lot, but he is also kind - perhaps how the rest of The Netherlands see the people of The Hague.

His very politically incorrect adventures often involve well-known personalities including the Royal Family, the Politicians, and of course all the ethnic groups who now live in The Hague

Map 10.4 – Back track around the fence to return to Grote Markt.

With Harry behind you, walk down the right-hand side of the square.

Map 10.5 – Take the first on the right to leave the Grote Markt by Vlamingstraat.

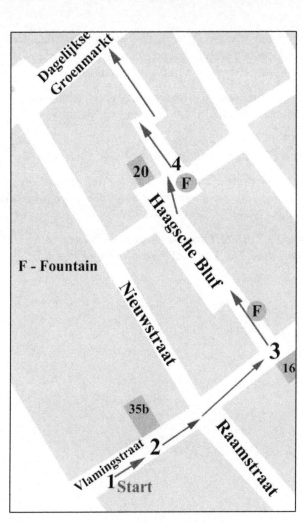

Map 11

Map 11.1 - Walk along to reach number 35b on your left.

35b Vlamingstraat

This is another pretty building. It uses yellow and blue bricks to make an eye-catching pattern.

Above the main door you can see some stone leaves and flowers. Between the first and second floor windows are two more sculptures, depicting transport and trade.

Right at the top are some stained glass windows, and above those you can just make out the head of Mercury watching over the street.

Map 11.2 - Keep walking along Vlamingstraat.

You will reach a crossroads with Nieuwstraat on your left and Raamstraat on your right. Make your way over the crossroads.

Map .3 - Turn left into the next little covered alley – it is just before number 16. You will arrive in Haagsche Bluf.

Haagsche Bluf

This is a redevelopment of a very old part of The Hague. The Hague is trying to revitalize the surviving old parts of the city, as well as retaining as much character as possible.

The pretty facades you see around this square are reproductions of old buildings in The Hague, some of which have been demolished, and some of which are still standing. Take a second look and you will see that they cleverly front much more boringly modern buildings.

The easiest reproduction to identify is number 20, which faces you at the far side of the square. It is a replica of the Page House, a listed building which you will see on Walk 2.

71

The square also boasts two French fountains from the eighteenth century, one against a wall and one in the middle of the square.

The name Haagsche Bluf comes from a traditional kind of egg-based dessert which is flavoured with berry juice.

There are several eateries here so you might want to consider it for a visit later in the evening.

Map 11.4 - Walk through the square, keeping more or less straight ahead.

You will exit onto Dagelijkse Groenmarkt, and right in front of you stands the Candy Box.

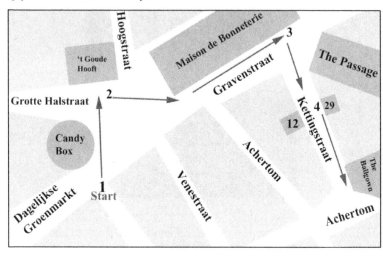

Map 12

The Candy Box

This spot has had many establishments built on it. There was once a convent here, it later became a meat market, and later some mansions were built

Things took a downturn in the twentieth century when a police station took up residence and later a steel and concrete

72

modern monstrosity. Thankfully it was removed and they put up this whimsical colourful building which the locals call The Candy Box.

Map 12.1 - Behind The Candy Box is an ornate inn known as 't Goude Hooft. Cross the busy road carefully to reach it.

't Goude Hooft

This is reputedly the oldest of The Hague's historic inns, so you could pop in if you need some refreshment.

It was built in the fifteenth century and was used by medieval business travelers from out of town. It was rebuilt in 1660 and the architect, Pieter Post, placed two golden heads on the façade for decoration - hence its name The Golden Head. You can see one golden head above you; the second is round the corner in Hoogstraat.

At the start of the twentieth century its owners planned to demolish it, as the building was in a sorry state by then. The Hague stepped in, bought it, and restored it to the original plans from the seventeenth century.

It reopened in 1939 – not the best year for business. It was renovated again in 2012 and is now a hotel once more

Map 12.2 - With 't Goude Hooft behind you, turn left along Grote Halstraat and follow the tram lines. You will walk into Gravenstraat.

The first building on your left is the Maison de Bonneterie, as it says on several plaques on the facade.

Maison de Bonneterie

As you walk past this building you can try to imagine its lost glory.

It was once The Hague's finest department store, however tastes change and it closed down in 2014. In contrast, Marks and Spencer opened a large store in The Hague on the same day!

However Maison de Bonneterie has been taken over recently and opened its doors once more. Luxury items are once again on sale.

Map 12.3 – Continue along the front of the store. Just before you reach the entrance of The Passage, turn right into Kettingstraat.

Kettingstraat was an old alley which was later widened to let the traffic pass through.

Pause when you reach number 29 on your left.

Kettingstraat 29

This is an example of Art Nouveau architecture by JW Bosboom.

It has a lovely little iron balcony on a blue and white tiled façade. To the right of the balcony you can read "De Goede Bron". Look right up to the top to see two more balconies and the lovely yellow floral art work.

Kettingstraat 12

Opposite it stands what was the first cinema in The Hague; it opened its doors in 1912. It later became a cabaret, then a nightclub, then back to be being a cinema. More recently it became a disco and is still used as a music venue.

It has a nice Art Nouveau canopy over the door.

Map 12.4 - Continue along Kettingstraat to reach a T-junction with Achterom. You will see The Ball Gown on your left.

The Ball Gown

This is one of The Hague's latest architectural stars. It is supposed to look like a ballerina wearing a ball gown. The ballerina even has a leg extended in ballerina pose at the corner.

Personally when I first saw it, I thought it was still wrapped in some sort of protective covering which would be peeled off at some future date. But no, this is the finished design – make your own mind up.

It has however regenerated this ancient and previously very run-down back alley of The Hague. Until quite recently, you simply would not have ventured into this part of town.

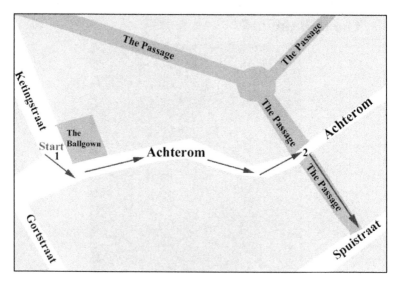

Map 13

Map 13.1 – Walk around the Ball Gown corner and into narrow and winding Achterom.

This is another of The Hague's oldest streets which was very run down until recently.

As you walk along, you should find it decorated with colourful and amusing murals of cats, all of which are connected by a very long ball of wool. The artwork was commissioned by the council to brighten this old street up – and I think they have succeeded.

Keep going to reach a crossroads.

Map 13.2 - You are now standing in the original Passage shopping centre which you explored earlier. Turn right to exit onto Spuistraat.

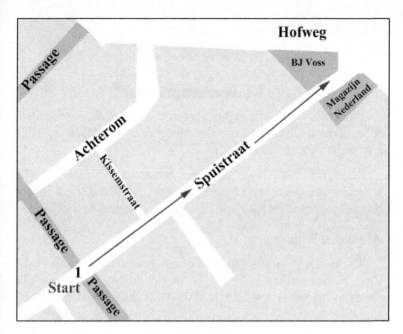

Map 14

Spuistraat

Spuistraat was where people went clothes shopping in the nineteenth century and it is still a busy shopping area.

A new extension to the Passage shopping centre has been built directly opposite the entrance to the old one. So, if you are in a shopping mode you could have a look. Just return to this point to continue the walk when you are finished.

Map 14.1 - With the original Passage entrance on your left, walk along Spuistraat, and eventually you will reach a T-junction with Hofweg.

The buildings at the end of Spuistraat on either side are worth a look.

Magazijn Nederland

The building on the right has some nice art deco decoration on the first floor, and "Magazijn Nederland" written in swirling gold letters above the corner door.

Magazijn Nederland was an Amsterdam company with branches all over the country. They were the first in the Netherlands to offer ready-made clothes – a brand new concept.

BJ Voss & Sons

The building on the left side of Spuistraat was owned by BJ Voss & Sons; they sold lady's and children's clothes. The company name is less obvious than Magazijn Nederland; it's engraved above the windows just before you exit Spuistraat.

The company was very proud of its beautiful new premises and boasted of an "Electric lift to all floors" in the adverts.

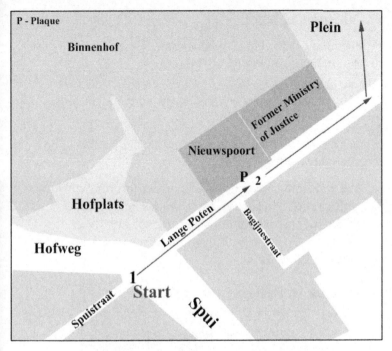

Map 15

Map 15.1 – With Spuistraat behind you, carefully cross Hofweg and then walk straight ahead into Lange Poten.

Lange Poten

This was just a sandy track back in the fourteenth century, and willow trees were planted along it. The willow trees have long since disappeared, and by the nineteenth century it had become one of the main shopping streets in The Hague. However new streets were being constructed and the shops and shoppers drifted away.

If you get a chance to play the Dutch version of Monopoly you will find Lange Poten on it.

Pass Bagijnestraat on your right. On your left you will see a bronze plaque beside the door of number 10.

79

Nieuwspoort

This building is the home to Nieuwspoort – as it says on the doors. In their own words:

"The only financially and politically independent press centre in the world.

We believe that journalists should always be able to do their work in freedom.

We welcome parliamentary reporters, information officers, political parties, trade unions, ministries, international organizations and civil society institutions. They are all given the space to present their news."

Plaque to Fallen Journalists

The plaque at the door of Nieuwspoort commemorates those journalists who were killed in WW2.

It depicts a falling figure holding onto a shield, and it represents the refusal of journalists to give up their freedom of speech, even when faced with death.

The poem on the plague is by Jan de Groot and translates as:

1940-1945

Hear!
The free word
Threatened, stifled
Brings forth its fighters
Produces its fighters
To the death.

Map 15.2 - Continue to the next building which is the former Ministry of Justice building.

Ministry of Justice

It held that grand title until the 1970's - if you look above the central door at number 42 you can see the title

Departement Justitie

Above that you will see two gentlemen staring down at you. They are famous Dutch lawyers from across the centuries. They are accompanied by four more lawyers around the corner.

These days this ornate building just holds government offices, as the Ministry of Justice has moved to much more modern premises.

A few more steps along Lange Poten will take you back into tree-filled Plein.

You have now reached the end of this walk.

Walk 2 – Museums and Canals

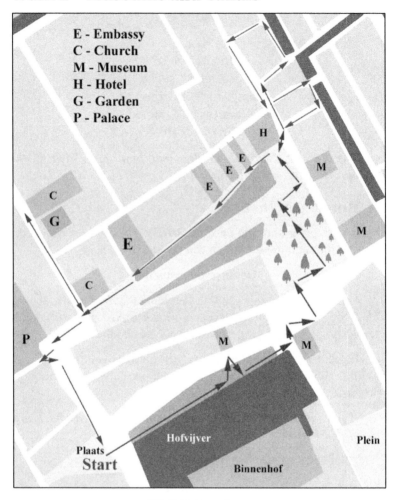

E - Embassy
C - Church
M - Museum
H - Hotel
G - Garden
P - Palace

Walk 2 Overview

This walk starts in Plaats, a triangular-shaped square near the Hofvijver Lake.

It takes in several museums before taking you to the canal-side and some nice old streets. You then walk through the embassy area to reach some interesting churches before returning to Plaats.

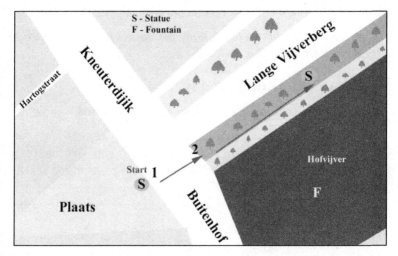

Map 1

Start at the Johan de Witt statue in Plaats which you saw on Walk 1. It stands just across the road from the little lake called Hofvijver.

Map 1.1 - Once you get there, cross the busy road.

Map 1.2 - Walk along the left-hand side of the lake which is lined by shady trees.

Along Hofvijver

This side of the lake gives you the best view of the Binnenhof, so take your time to enjoy it.

The Hofvijver was just a little pond when the first hunting lodge was built, but when the lodge was converted into a castle the pond was enlarged.

All that excavated sand was dumped on this side of the lake. It was soon packed down into a useable road, and wealthy families who wanted to be near the seat of power built their

83

houses here. Unfortunately none of those old houses survived the centuries, and we are left with the eighteenth century houses which run along the left side of the lake which you see today.

After about 100 meters along the lakeside you will see a statue in a little garden under the trees.

Johan van Oldenbarnevelt

This is Johan van Oldenbarnevelt who you read about on walk 1.

He was the statesman who was tried and executed by decapitation when he and Prince Maurits failed to agree on the future path of The Netherlandds.

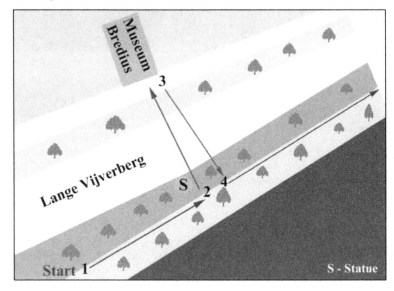

Map 2

Map 2.1 - Continue along under the trees. After another 100 meters you will find another statue.

Jantje (Little John)

This one is a young boy named Jantje. He was the son of Count Floris V, the count who first built a hunting lodge here and founded The Hague.

The children of The Hague have a little song they sing about this statue. The words are etched into the wall which stands in front of the statue, and they translate as:

> In The Hague there lives a Count
> and his son is called Jantje
> If you ask: 'Where does your daddy live?'
> He'll point with this hand.
> With his finger and his thumb
> On his hat he wears a feather
> On his arm's a basket
> Bye, my sweet Jantje!

Jantje is answering the question in the song; he is pointing to the Binnenhof across the lake where his father would have been.

It's supposed to be lucky to shake his hand, and you can see his bronze finger and thumb are shining from the constant rubbing.

Little Jantje became Count of Holland himself at the tender age of 13 when his father died. He died just two years later.

Map 2.2 - Stand face to face with Jantje. Behind Jantje stands the Museum Bredius.

Museum Bredius

This little museum is worth a visit if you have bought one of the combination museum tickets.

Abraham Bredius came from a family which made its fortune in the gunpowder trade. He spent his fortune on his beloved art collection and later became the director of the Mauritshuis and was known as an expert on Rembrandt.

The house holds his personal collection.

If you don't want to visit the Museum Bredius, continue this walk from "Towards the Haags Historisch Museum"on page 89.

Otherwise make your way to the museum door.

You can explore the three floors and enjoy its treasures and period furniture.

Bust of Christ - Rembrandt

As a passionate expert on Rembrandt, it's only fitting that Bredius owned one. This painting is part of a series of nine "Busts of Christ" which are in museums all over the world.

No-one knows if Rembrandt used a model or his imagination for the face of Christ.

It should be mentioned that some experts doubt Rembrandt actually painted any of them, and that they were probably exercise pieces for his students.

Another painting worth searching for is:

Scene on the ice outside the town walls - Aert van der Neer

It shows us a wintery scene with the townspeople assembling for a game of ice-hockey on the frozen lake.

Perspective Box

On the top landing is an interesting triangular device known as a perspective box. This is one of only six which are known to have survived.

An image of a room sits inside the box, but if viewed normally it looks disjointed and all wrong. It was drawn so that when you look at it through the peephole situated at the front of the box, your eye will turn it into a 3D image – extremely clever for the age it was produced in.

Map 2.3 - When you exit the museum return to the lakeside.

Towards the Haags Historisch Museum

Map 2.4 – Face the lake and turn left to reach its end.

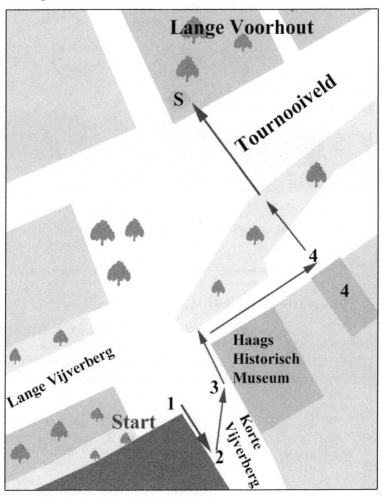

Map 3

When you reach the end of the lake you will see Haags Historisch Museum in front of you.

Map 3.1 - Before going in, turn right to see the best view of the lake.

Facing the lake, and on your left, is the back of the lovely Maruitshuis and the little Torentje where the prime-minister works.

Map 3.2 – Cross Korte Vijverberg to reach the Museum.

Haags Historisch Musuem

There are many interesting items in this museum, especially those paintings which show us The Hague from previous centuries. It makes you realise just how much of The Hague was lost during the devastation of World War II and later replaced by modern skyscrapers.

Note, items from the permanent exhibition do get swapped in and out depending on what else is on show. Here are some personal favourites which you might find:

View of The Hague from the southeast - Jan van Goyen

This huge painting presents you with a slightly elevated view of The Hague. Spot the tower of the Grote Kerk. The large building to the right of the tower is of course the Knights Hall. This painting used to hang in the old Town Hall which you saw on walk 1.

The Hofvijver seen from the Target Field – Adam van Breen

This painting is interesting, not just because you see The Hague from long ago, but because it's painted from more or less where you are right now.

On the left of the lake is the Binnenhof, on the right is the tree lined Lange Vijverberg which you have just walked along. At the other end you can see the original village of Den Haag huddled around the Grote Kerk. It's clearly winter, as the townspeople are enjoying skating on the lake.

The Hofvijver seen from Korte Vijverberg – Paulus Constantijn

A later view across the Hofvijver again painted from where you are now. The Binnenhof is much grander in this painting, and everyone seems much more prosperous.

Willem Jansz - Standard-bearer - Everard Crijnsz

With frills around the neck, shoes with little bows, feathers and ribbons, and of course the yellow veil draped over the shoulder – it's quite an outfit.

The chap in this painting was the son of a successful cloth merchant, and as it is a ceremonial outfit we can give him a bit of leeway. He would certainly stand out in a crowd.

Alexandrine Tinne - Henri Auguste d'Ainecy Montpezat

This lady was the daughter of a wealthy Dutch merchant, and when her elderly father died she was the richest heiress in the Netherlands. With all that money she and her mother set off to see the world.

They travelled first to Norway, Italy, Egypt and the Middle East and then got more adventurous. She and her mother were the first European women to travel up the White Nile, but then Alexandrine fell ill, meaning they could venture no further and they returned to Khartoum.

Undeterred they set out again once she recovered and explored Africa - her mother died of fever on one of those trips. Alexandrine stayed in Africa and travelled extensively, collecting plants as she explored – she has many named after her.

In 1869 she tried to reach the Tuareg people in the Sahara, but her party was attacked by the very Tuareg she so desperately wanted to meet. Alexandrine was cut by a sword and bled to death - a truly sad ending for such an interesting woman of that time. There is a memorial in deepest Sudan listing her as one of the great explorers of Africa, and a plaque in Tangiers commemorates her.

Portrait of Prince William and Mary I Stuart - Gerard van Honthorst

The young couple is William II of Orange, and Mary Stuart, the daughter of King Charles I of Great Britain - and they are very, very young, he is 14 and she is just 10. Of course it was a political marriage to form an alliance against Spain.

She was the first "Princess Royal", setting the traditional title for the oldest daughter of the monarch.

Theirs is another sad story though, William died at just 24 of smallpox, and Mary at 29 also of smallpox.

The De Witt brothers' body parts

If you remember the story of Johan de Witt from Walk 1, you can view a much more gruesome exhibit - a preserved tongue and finger from either Cornelius or Johan de Witt – no-one knows which. They are in a little glass coffin.

Map 3.3 - Leave the museum. Turn right to reach busy Tournooiveld which has tramlines running along it.

Turn right along Tournooiveld to reach number 4 on your right.

On the other side of Tournooiveld is what looks like a park, but it is in fact a long wide tree-filled street which is called Lange Voorhout.

Lange Voorhout

It was farmland in the middle ages but was bought up by statesmen and politicians who built their mansions along its edges.

It was Emperor Charles V who then ordered that it should be filled with the lovely Linden trees you see – he was inspired by the linden trees on Berlin's famous street, Unter den Linden.

Map 3.4 – Cross Tournoieveld to reach the trees. You will see a rather odd monument on the left-hand side of the trees.

Thorbecke Monument

It consists of two separate statues.

Thorbecke was a politician in the nineteenth century. He campaigned tirelessly to transfer power from the crown to parliament.

Eventually the King conceded and Thorbecke played a key role in writing the new constitution. The King appointed Thorbecke as head of the first Council, effectively making him the first prime minister of the Netherlands. He then spent most of his life here in The Hague as a politician, and was officially prime minister three times.

His monument shows him at the back, sitting at a marble desk with his head turned and looking across the lake to the seat of power.

In front of him is another statue. It is made of a much more modern material, representing the modern state he helped to create. It shows us citizens discussing and arguing freely. The artist is quoted as saying:

> "Having the woman seated on top of the table is my way of showing how her place in society has become equal."

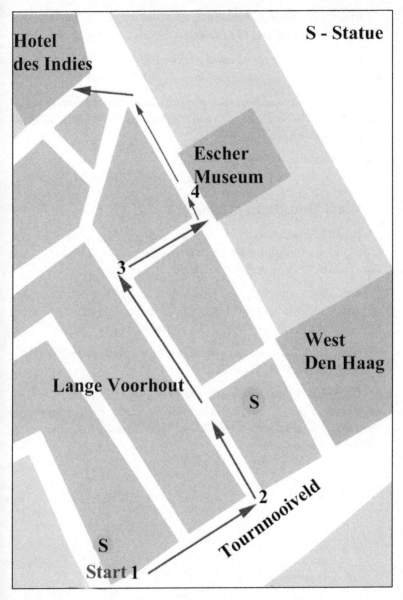

Map 4

Map 4.1 – Face the statue and turn right to walk along Tournooiveld keeping the Linden trees on your left.

Map 4.2 - Take the second pathway on your left through the trees.

You will reach a towering monument to Prince Bernhard of Saxe-Weimar-Eisenach on your right – he is one of Holland's military heroes.

If you are exploring on Thursday or Sunday you might find an antique and book market going on.

West Den Haag Museum

Behind Prince Bernhard is one of the ugliest buildings you will find in this old part of The Hague. It was originally the American Embassy and it was strictly off limits.

The diplomats have moved out now and a museum has moved in. So if you are interested in contemporary or modern art you might want to have a look to see what's on.

Map 4.3 - To continue this walk, stand with both the statue and the museum on your right.

Continue along the pathway through the trees. As you approach a path junction, you will spot the Escher museum with its very distinctive facade on your right. Make your way over to the museum.

Escher Museum

The Escher collection is housed in this lovely building, the one-time Winter Palace of Queen Mother Emma of the Netherlands. As you wander around you can read about how the various rooms were used by the royal family.

When Escher displayed his works, the public loved the eccentricity of them. If you visit you can stand amused or bemused in front of over 150 examples. They tend to fall into two broad categories, impossible constructions, and optical illusions.

The top floor is the most popular with younger visitors, because you can interact with some of Escher's ideas. There is usually a crowd of teenagers around the disintegrating floor, but my personal favourite is the bottomless pit – you will know it when you look down.

Chandeliers

As you explore don't miss the chandeliers specially designed for the museum.

When you reach the ballroom, you will find the Star Chandelier reflected endlessly in two mirrors. You can of course take a photograph of yourself reflected endlessly in the same mirrors.

Here are some favourite Escher works to find:

Sky and Water

The fish and birds fit together like a jigsaw puzzle. So when you look at the middle of the picture, you can see both depending on whether you look at the white or the black shapes – try switching your focus from one to the other.

Belvedere

This one will make your head hurt if you try to make sense of it. Look at the pillars on the middle floor and you will see that the back pillars are actually connected to the front wall and vice versa. The ladder does the same trick; it switches from the front of the house to the back of the house as it rises. Our brains try to turn it into a three dimensional image, but it can't sort out those pillars because they are impossible in 3D,

Ascending and Descending

This is another example of the brain trying to sort out what the eye is telling it. The stairway at the top is never-ending and those men are never going to get to the top or bottom.

When your head can't take any more, leave the museum.

Map 4.4 – Stand facing away from the museum and turn right.

You will see the Hotel des Indies ahead of you, so make your way towards it.

Hotel des Indes

This lovely hotel was built as a family home for Baron van Brienen in the nineteenth century.

It became a hotel in 1881 and some very famous people have stayed here, including Sir Winston Churchill, Czar Nicholas of Russia, Emperor Haile Selassie of Ethiopia, and much more recently, Prince. The famous ballerina Anna Pavlova stayed here, but she also died here – she caught pneumonia.

The hotel was one of Europe's finest – until World War I changed Europe completely. The hotel was bought and about to be turned into offices – but the then mayor of The Hague intervened and The Hague bought it.

The hotel struggled along between the wars even surviving a fire. World War II was no kinder than World War I and the hotel housed the German command.

After the war the decline continued until quite recently when real money was put into renovating and improving it. The hotel was completely renovated in 2006 and is now one of the best in town.

Hague's canals

Most of The Hague's central canals have long gone, but you will now visit a nearby little corner where there are some survivors. It is also full of shops, cafes and restaurants and is a nice spot to stop for a bit of lunch or a coffee.

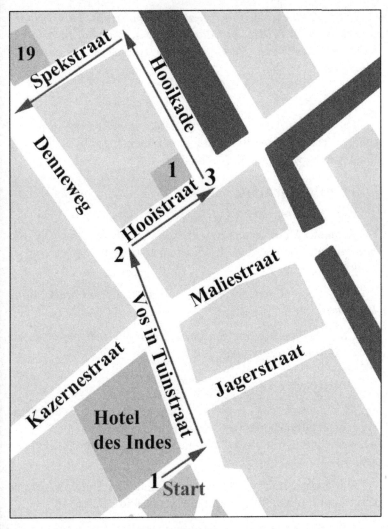

Map 5

Map 5.1 - Face the Hotel des Indes, and go round its right-hand side into Vos In Tuinstraat. Pass Jagerstraat and Maliestraat on your right.

103

Map 5.2 - Take the third right into Hooistraat. This will take you to a canal bridge, but don't cross it. Instead turn left to walk into Hooikade. Pause at the first house at the corner of Hooikade.

Hooikade 1

This used to be an old livery stable, but it has been mostly rebuilt. However the livery stable is remembered by the horse's head which greets you above the door.

The Hooigracht

The canal which runs along the street is called the Hooigracht. Hooi means hay and this canal was how hay was brought into The Hague. It was then sold on the street you are walking along now.

Map 5.3 – Face the canal and turn left to walk along Hooikade.

Take the first left into Spekstraat, and you will soon reach a T-junction with Denneweg.

Denneweg

This is another of the oldest streets in The Hague. The name was originally Duineweg, which translates as Dune Road, because long ago it meandered along the dunes which filled this area.

These days it is where you will find The Hague's antique shops, but it is also full of designer shops and cafes.

Take a look at the building on your right; it sits on the corner of Spekstraat and Denneweg.

Denneweg 19

This building once housed the largest cigar maker in The Netherlands.

Take a look at the wooden heads carved above the windows. They are native people of the America's where tobacco came from.

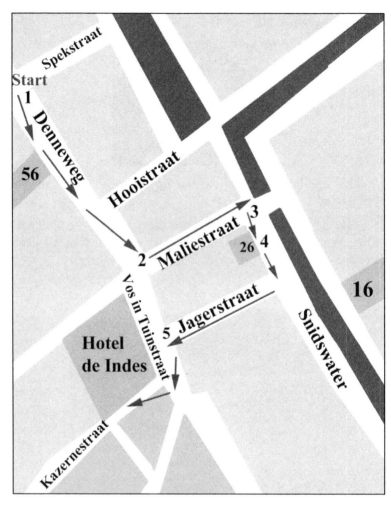

Map 6

Map 6.1 - Face the old cigar shop and turn right along Denneweg to reach number 56 on your right.

Denneweg 56

It's a beautiful Art Nouveau building in glass and cast iron. It was built at the end of the nineteenth century for a blacksmith, so it is fitting that it contains 45,000 kg of iron.

If you remember exploring Haagsche Bluf on Walk 1, one of the lovely reproduced facades which you saw was of this building; although the reproduction is in white, as this building was originally.

Map 6.2 – Continue along Denneweg. Pass Hooistraat on your left, then turn left into Maliestraat. You will approach another canal.

Map 6.3 – Turn right to walk along the canal edge on Smidswater. Pause at number 26.

Huis van Lorrie

This building was designed by the architect JPJ Lorrie as his own home. It's thought that he decided to use it as an advertisement for his skills, and did so by designing the left half in gothic style, and the right half in Art Nouveau style.

The Gothic half is decorated with two little gargoyles flanking the first floor windows. Look up and you will see two larger gargoyles looking down at you.

The Art Nouveau half has a beautiful bay window.

Don't miss the very pretty golden Art Nouveau letterbox. It's decorated with a very stylized cat which has a doorbell button for a nose.

The writing below the letter box translates as

"For letters, don't ring!"

Map 6.4 – Walk to the next corner with Jagerstraat.

Mata Hari

Look over the canal and slightly to the right to see where Mata Hari lived at the very start of her infamous career. It's number 16 and has dark green shutters. It was actually her uncle's house.

It looks disappointingly respectable for the home of the famous exotic dancer and WWI double spy. Mata Hari was executed in 1917 by a French firing squad. An eye witness reported that she was not blindfolded or tied up in any way, and that she blew a kiss to the gunmen just before they fired.

There is a plaque to commemorate her infamous residence, but it has been placed just to the left of the front door. If the green shutters are open, as they usually are, you cannot actually see the plaque, so there is no point in getting any closer.

Now turn into Jagerstreet to reach a T-junction with Vos In Tuinstraat.

Map 6.5 - Turn left into Vos in Tuinstraat, and then next right to return to the front of the Hotel des Indes.

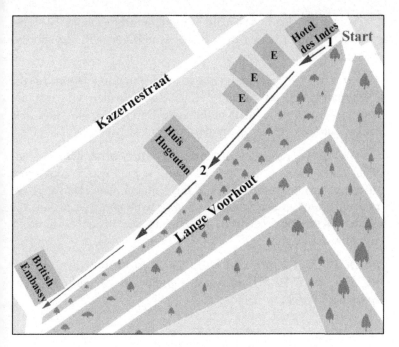

Map 7

Embassies

Map 7.1 - Face the door of the Hotel des Indes and turn left along Lange Voorhout.

You now have a pleasant walk along this tree-shaded road through the Embassy quarter.

Walk past the Embassies of Spain, Angola, and Switzerland – all displaying their flags just to let everyone know who is who.

Just past the embassies stands the rather grand Huis Huguetan at number 34.

Huis Huguetan

It was built in the eighteenth century for Adriana Margaretha Huguetan, the daughter of a very wealthy banker.

A century later it became the temporary home of King William I until Kneuterdijk Palace (which you will see shortly) was ready for his arrival.

After that it became home to the Supreme Court of the Netherlands, known as the "Hoge Raad" which you can see engraved above the main door. The Supreme Court has now moved out to much larger modern premises.

The Hague has been dithering on what to do with it since then. First it was a museum and then the plan was to move part of the government into it while the Binnenhof is renovated. So you will have to see what is actually happening when you get there. With luck you will be able to see inside as it has a sumptuous interior.

Map 7.2 - Continue towards the end of this street and you will find the British Embassy at number 10 – usually sporting some Union Jacks.

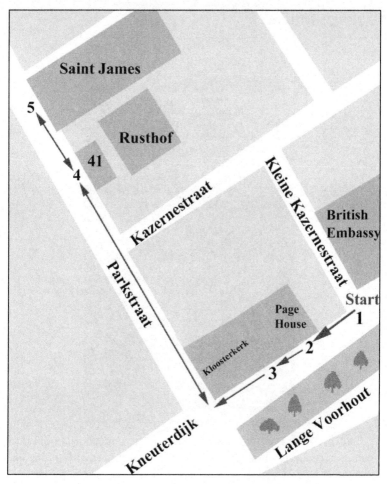

Map 8

Map 8.1 - Once past the British embassy, cross Kleine Kazernestraat.

A few more steps will bring you to the Page House, brightly decorated with its red shuttered windows.

Page House

At one time a monastery attached to the church just next door stood here, but when the monastery was destroyed this house was built as a private home.

The house was later called the Page House because it was where the Pages of the Prince of Orange were housed until 1828.

It's one of the few stepped gabled houses left in The Hague, and you will probably notice that it's not symmetrical. If you look up you can see two plaques - the God of War Mars, and his mother Bellona. They mark the boundary of the original house – the extra bit on the left hand side was added much later

The Red Cross moved in in the nineteenth century and the house was modernised – but since then it has been restored and an attempt made to return it to its original character. It's only open for visits on Heritage Days so you need to be satisfied with the colourful exterior.

Map 8.2 – Walk a little further along to find the entrance to the Kloosterkerk.

Kloosterkerk

This church and its adjoining monastery were built in the fourteenth century. It was stripped during the iconoclasm in the sixteenth century and the monks fled. The church was left to fall apart and was only saved because it was turned into a cannon foundry and ammunition store. Unfortunately the ammunition exploded in the seventeenth century leaving the monastery more or less destroyed. The church survived but its military role continued – in 1813 a Cossack regiment was billeted here.

The church was ear-marked for demolition and was only saved when the Dutch Reformed Church moved in. It has now been restored and is still in use today.

If it's open, pop in to have a look around as there are a couple of interesting items to find.

Apostle chapel

The Apostle chapel has an impressive stained glass window dedicated to the twelve apostles. Each is shown holding a symbol with which the apostle is usually associated.

Top row:

Matthew (scroll)
Thaddaeus (spear)
Paul (sword)
Philip (inverted cross)
Simon Zelotes (saw)
James the Less (club)

Bottom row:

Andrew (saltire-cross)
Peter (church on a rock)
John (book)
James (sword)
Thomas (book)
Bartholomew (knife)

There is also a very modern mosaic of The Last Supper.

The Atlantic Wall

Both the window and the mosaic were originally in the Duinoord Church. In 1942 the Germans ordered the demolition of that church and also many buildings around it to make way for the "Atlantic Wall". It was a line of forts and walls built to hold the Allied Armies back.

The parishioners immediately set to work, and managed to extract the mosaic (which weighs 12,000 kilograms"), the apostle window and several other items before the diggers moved in. They hid them in the Peace Palace garden. They were installed here in this church after the war.

Radar Love

George Kooymans came from The Hague and was guitarist and singer with the rock band Golden Earring.

In 2021 Kooymans had to retire due to illness, so a tribute to his work with Golden Earring was held here. Their greatest hit Radar Love was played on the organ!

Daniel Farenheit

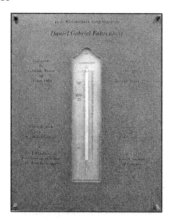

Farenheit was actually German although he was born in Gdansk in Poland. He then spent most of his life in Holland.

He moved to The Hague in 1717 where he came up with his greatest invention, the thermometer. He died in The Hague and was buried in this church.

In 2009 this interesting memorial was unveiled by the Polish ambassador to mark his grave.

De Ruyter

You will also see a bell attached to one of the church walls. It was the bell of the De Rueyter, a Dutch cruiser which was torpedoed by the Japanese navy off the cost of Java in 1942. The ship sank with the loss of over 300 of her crew.

There is a commemoration service held every year in February.

> Note, there are often Bach concerts here, so check when you visit to see if there is something on which appeals to you.

When you exit the church, take a little diversion to see one of The Hague's old almshouses.

Map 8.3 – Take a few steps to reach the corner of the church and turn right into Parkstraat. Pass Kazernestraat on your right and find number 41, also on your right.

You will find an anonymous door with Rusthof written on it. Push through and you will enter the garden of The Rusthof

Rusthof

This beautiful garden belongs to the Rusthof almshouse. It was started by a devout protestant couple to help the poor of The Hague. This almshouse was for elderly single and destitute women – in those days, elderly was over 55!!!

The benefactors also built a sewing school which sits in the garden – its purpose was to teach sewing so the residents could make some money on their own - the school only closed in 1930. It was renovated in the eighties when the houses were all modernised.

Of course you must be quiet and not disturb the current residents. They occasionally arrange events here - one Christmas there was a carol concert with fire pits and gluhwein. They do appreciate a little donation to keep the garden beautiful, so if you appreciate the garden you can drop a few euros into the collection box near the door.

Map 8.4 - When you leave the Rusthof, turn right to find the church of Saint James just next door.

St. James the Greater

The church boasts the second highest tower in The Hague and the largest organ in the Netherlands.

The Labyrinth

If the gate is open, you can try out the labyrinth which is on the courtyard outside the church.

At the centre is a stone which bears a Christ monogram, so the labyrinth is supposed to teach us that all roads lead to Christ.

Inside the church

Inside is very pretty and is worth a visit but the church is often closed. If you do get in, take a close look at the lovely altar and the unusual pulpit.

If you happen to be there around 4:00 pm you might find an organ concert in full swing, making the most of the huge organ. It's free so you could have a rest while you listen.

Map 8.5 - Backtrack to return to the corner of the Kloosterkerk and the T junction with Lange Voorhoot.

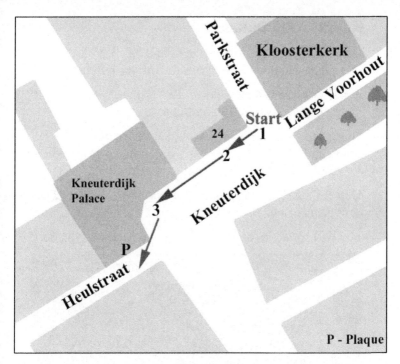

Map 9

Map 9.1 - Turn right to continue into Kneuterdijk. You will find number 24 on your right-hand side almost immediately.

Kneuterdijk 24

This huge building belonged to Johan van Oldenbarnevelt. He was the statesman who was beheaded in the Binnenhof, and who you read about on Walk 1 (Page 24).

He built his wonderful new home in 1611, but he didn't enjoy it for very long as he was executed in 1619. These days it holds a government office.

Map 9.2 - Continue in the same direction.

As the road bends left you will find yourself outside Kneuterdijk Palace on the right-hand corner.

Kneuterdijk Palace

This was one of the royal palaces and has been used off-and-on over the last couple of centuries for various purposes.

When war trials were held in The Netherlands after WWII, they were held in its beautiful ballroom.

The palace was renovated in 2012. It is now used by the government, so you can only visit on Heritage Days when the public gets access to buildings normally off limits.

Map 9.3 - Facing the palace, go round the left-hand side to leave by Heulstraat.

You will see a plaque on the side of the palace as you do.

The plaque commemorates the handing of the right to vote and elect parliament to the people, rather than leaving the king to do it. That discussion and decision took place in the palace. It translates as:

King Willem 2nd and his advisers
discussed decisively changes to The Netherlands constitution
in this house 1847.

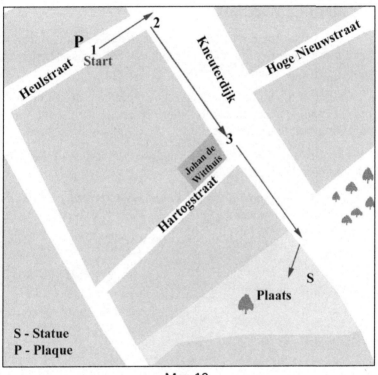

Map 10

NOTE. You have almost reached the end of walk 2. If you have time and energy, you could tackle Walk 3 which starts from this point. If you wish to do so, continue from Page 123.

Finishing Walk 2

Map 10.1 - Backtrack along Heulstraat to the junction with Kneuterdijk.

Map 10.2 – Turn right into Kneuterdijk and walk along until you reach number 6 on your right. It stands at the corner of Kneuterdijik and Hartogstraat.

Johan de Witthuis

This stately home is where Johan de Witt lived at one time – very close to where he and his brother were assassinated by a mob.

Calling it his home is a bit of a grand claim as Johan de Witt only actually lived there for three years, but it's the only surviving building where he did live, so it's the only contender.

There is a plaque below the windows to the left of the door commemorating his stay.

Map 10.3 – Continue along Kneuterdijk to return to Plaats on your right-hand side.

You have now reached the end of this walk.

Walk 3 – Palaces and Stables

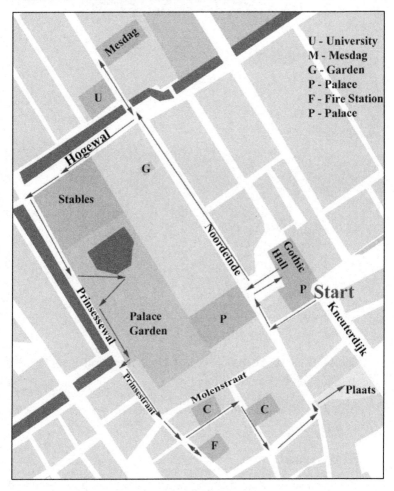

U - University
M - Mesdag
G - Garden
P - Palace
F - Fire Station
P - Palace

Walk 3 Overview

This walk takes you along Noordiende, one of the most interesting streets in The Hague for both history and shops.

It then takes you to the Mesdag Panaorama Museum and then back into town via the Royal Stables and the Palace Park.

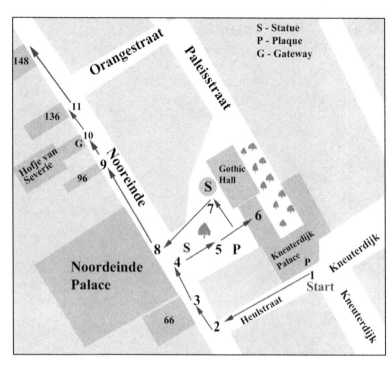

Map 1

The walk starts at the corner of Heulstraat and Kneuterdijk, just outside the Kneuterdijk Palace.

Map 1.1 – Walk along Heulstraat to reach a T-junction with Nooreinde.

Heulstraat

The Haagse Beek used to run down Nooreinde passing where you are standing now. Heulstraat got its name from a "huel", a wooden bridge which stood here and which was used to cross the Haagse Beek. No need for that now, as the Beek has long gone.

Map 1.2 - Turn right into Nooreinde and you will find number 66 on your left.

Nooreinde 66

This is where the current King used to live before his mother abdicated and he took on the throne. His name is King Willem-Alexander and the little posts of the railing outside are adorned with his initials WA.

Map 1.3- A little further on you will reach an impressive equestrian statue of William the Silent who is facing Noordeinde Palace.

Noordeinde Palace

This is the working palace of the monarch – you can see the royal coat of arms on the gates. If you want to know whether the king is in the office, look for the Royal Flag. If it's up he is working, and if it's down he is somewhere else.

At the top of the palace gates you can see the Royal coat of arms declaring "Je Maintiendrai", or "I will maintain".

The palace started as just a medieval farmhouse which was bought by the stewards of Holland in the sixteenth century. It has been enlarged and restyled over the years.

It's been host to many famous visitors. In the eighteenth century the French writer Voltaire was a visitor, and much more recently President Putin of Russia was a guest.

If you were able to visit you could see the original farmhouse cellars in the basement – but of course it's strictly off limits except for a few days in summer.

Map 1.4 - Walk into the little square behind William the Silent. You will see a large tree with a bench running around it.

The Stamp Tree

This White Chestnut tree was planted in the late nineteenth century and it got its nickname because The Hague's stamp collectors used to gather beneath it to swap stamps. It had to be rescued in 1990 by a tree surgeon, but is now healthy again.

Map 1.5 – Behind the Stamp Tree you will find the steps which will take you down to the entrance to the Gothic Hall

The Gothic Hall

It is part of Kneuterdijk Palace which you saw the other side of a short while ago.

It was added by King William II when he stayed in the palace as crown prince. He had the hall built in Tudor style.

It is not always open but if you are lucky do go in to see it. You will see it still has its wooden gothic roof and some stained glass windows, but to be honest it's not a patch on how it was originally, which you can see below.

While you are there you could step into the little garden which sits behind the Kneuterdijk Palace.

Map 1.6 - Make your way back towards the Stamp Tree, but turn right before you reach it to spot another Royal Statue

Queen Wilhelmina

This one shows a surprising resemblance to a Womble. However, it depicts the much respected Queen Wilhelmina, as she and her family fled their homeland for the United Kingdom when the Nazis invaded in 1940.

Queen Wilhelmina was The Netherlands longest reigning monarch, through both WWI and WWII. She became the leader of the Dutch Government in exile and spoke to her people often via radio and she was seen as an inspiration to the Dutch resistance. Radio Orange was banned and the people had to listen secretly at night to hear their queen.

Turn round to face the same way as Queen Wilhelmina.

Opposite the statue is a paved compass, and behind that is a plaque which shows the respect the Dutch people had for their queen. It reads:

Behind her voice from exile
was a figure like this

She was awarded the Order of the Garter by the United Kingdom and Churchill is said to have described her as:

"The only real man
among the governments-in-exile in London"

Map 1.7 - Return to the statue of William the Silent, and then cross the road to the Palace gates.

Map 1.8 - Turn right to walk along Noordeinde.

Once you get past the Palace, you will find that Noordeinde is definitely a street for window shopping. It's full of unusual little shops and well worth a browse around.

Stop for a look at number 96 on your left.

Noordeinde 96

This pretty building was built at the start of the nineteenth century for D. Sala en Zonen; he was an art dealer.

He specialised in the works of the three brothers Jacob, Matthijs and Willem Maris – part of The Hague School of Painters. To celebrate this connection, three stone portraits of the brothers were added on the top floor surrounding the little balcony. The building is called the Marishuis by the locals.

Map 1.9 - Continue along Noordeinde until you reach a small gateway between numbers 102 and 122.

Step through the gateway you will reach a seventeenth century courtyard, the Hofje van Severie.

Hofje van Severie

These days it's a little oasis of calm, but it used to hold a row of very small one-room houses. The old rooms had a shared external toilet and water pump – very basic. Those have been replaced with the more modern buildings you see today.

Map 1.10 - Continue along Noordeinde to reach number 136 on your left.

Noordeinde 136

This is another example of Art Nouveau. Look up to see the two lovely balconies, and between them a bay window.

Map 1.11 - Keep going, passing Oranjestraat your right. Stop at number 148 on your left.

Noordeinde 148

This is another art dealer's establishment from long ago which is now a bar. It was built in 1912, and on the first floor are two lions on either side of the building holding shields confirming that date, Anno 1912.

The owner clearly wanted to make his building beautiful. Above the door is Saint George on horseback fighting a dragon, and above the saint is the motto of the art dealer which roughly translates as:

"In the past, the present, in the present it will become,"

Looking further up you can see that all the windows are filled with elderly stained glass.

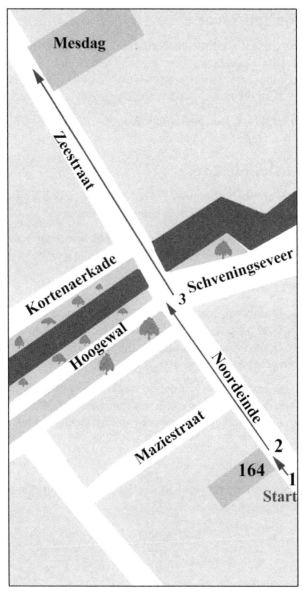

Map 2

Map 2.1 - Continue to reach number 164 on your left.

130

Noordeinde 164

This is another one for lovers of Art Nouveau. It has a lovely tiled panel at the entrance.

Map 2.2 - Continue along Noordeinde and you will pass Maziestraat on your left. Eventually you will reach a crossroads with a canal and a busy road.

Map 2.3 - Cross both to walk into Zeestraat. A short walk will bring you to Mesdag on the right hand side at number 65.

Mesdag Panorama

Panorama paintings were very popular with the public in the nineteenth century, and Mesdag was commissioned to paint a panorama in 1880.

He was a marine painter and he and his team produced a 360 degree painting of the nearby seaside village of Scheveningen with The Hague in the background. In 1886 the company which owned it went bust, so Mesdag took the business over, paid its debts, and it is still owned by the same family. It's the only surviving Panorama in the world.

You walk through a gallery of some of Mesdag's more conventional paintings as you approach the Panorama, and you will see that marine paintings were his passion. Finally, you will walk through a little dark passage and up a spiral staircase and emerge into a dome and the effect is quite astonishing.

Your horizon is filled with a view of the sea, and the shore is populated with nineteenth century people and places. As you walk around the viewing platform, try to identify The Hague in the distance.

When you leave the Panorama and return downstairs, you have the chance of viewing an interesting twenty minute film on how the Panorama was recently saved and restored. Just ask one of the staff for the English version.

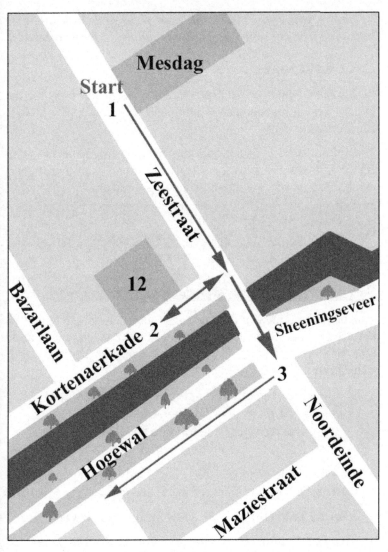

Map 3

Map 3.1 - When you leave Mesdag, turn left to return to the canal you crossed earlier.

Before you cross the canal, turn right and walk along to reach the first door on your right at number 12 Kortenaerkade.

12 Kortenaerkade

This is a beautiful Art Deco building originally built for the Dutch Telephone company, although it is now part of the Erasmus University.

Right at the top of the building are four enigmatic Egyptian figures, holding an owl, a staff, a train, and a hammer, symbolising peace, invention, technology, and art.

Above the door you can see some poetry in golden letters by the Dutch poet Boutens - the words celebrate communication which is very fitting for a communications company. It translates roughly as

> Spoken or written, the Word borrows
> the wings of his mother, the Thought,
> and rushes, still, for days and nights
> to his destination

On either side of those words lies a lady sending a message by carrier pigeon, and a man receiving that message.

Map 3.2 - Backtrack to the canal bridge and cross it.

Map 3.3 – Turn right into Hogewal and walk about 100 meters to pass the first block on your left.

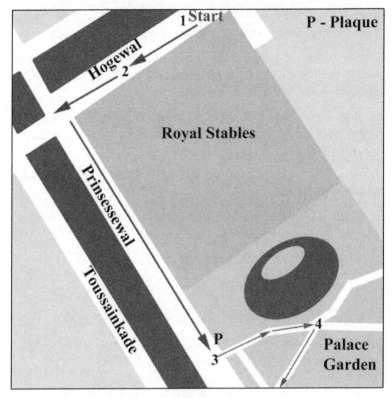

Map 4

Map 4.1 - Continue along Hogewal and the next block you will reach is the front of the enormous Royal Stables.

Royal Stables

The stables were built, as it proclaims at the top of the building, in 1878. This is where the carriages, horses, and cars used to transport the royal family are kept.

This includes the Golden Coach which was given to Queen Wilhelmina by the people when she took the throne at just 18. It is made of teak, covered in gold leaf, and decorated with ornate symbols. It has a raised roof in the centre because Queen Wilhelmina insisted that she must be able to stand upright in it.

It is used on Prince's Day when the monarch travels to the Ridderzaal to give the budget speech from the throne. It's a great occasion in The Netherlands.

The Royal Stables are open to the public only for a short time in summer. So you might be lucky and find you can visit and see the coaches.

Map 4.2 – Continue to the end of the Stables, then turn left into Prinsessewal.

Walk along the side of the canal on Prinsessewal to reach the Palace Garden which sits just beyond the Stables.

Stop at the first park gate on your left.

Palace Garden

The Palace Garden's real name is the Princess Garden.

It was founded by Louise de Coligny who was the fourth wife and widow of William I of Orange, and there is a plaque at the gate about it.

The park is usually open to the public, unless there is an official engagement taking place. From the gateway you can see the tall tower of St James the Greater peeping over the trees.

Map 4.3 - Enter the park and walk straight ahead to reach a crossroads in front of the park's pond.

If you are visiting in spring you may see the lawns covered in brightly coloured crocus.

The park has its place in history. It was from this little park that Jean-Pierre Blanchard took off in the first manned hot-air balloon launched from the Netherlands, as depicted in this painting by G. Carbentus.

Blanchard landed in Zevenhuizen near Gouda where the local peasants attacked and destroyed the balloon, probably because they had never seen such a thing before.

Map 4.4 - Face away from the pond.

Take the right hand path which leads diagonally away from the pond and towards the park wall.

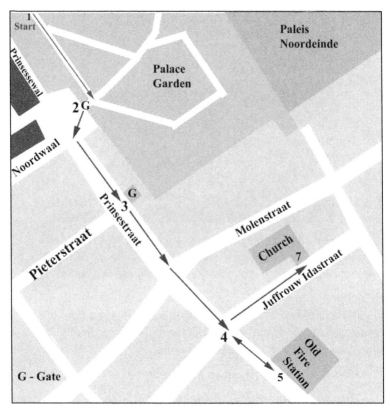

Map 5

Map 5.1 - When you reach the park wall, turn left keeping the wall on your right-hand side.

Exit the park by a second gate. It lies about 100 meters further along.

Map 5.2 - With that gate behind you, turn left to leave the canals behind, and head back into town along Prinsestraat.

Prinsestraat is another of The Hague's oldest streets.

Pause at a very old brick gateway on your left between numbers 73 and 75.

Old Gateway

This elderly and rather neglected gateway was built in the seventeenth century. It's believed that it once gave access to the Palace Garden you have just visited, but was later disconnected by the houses built around it.

It's also said that it was used as a secret exit by the Prince, to escape the Paleis Noordeinde and disappear into the city for a break – what a lovely idea. It's just a shame it's so neglected.

Map 5.3 - Continue along Prinsestraat. Pass Molenstraat to reach Juffrouw Idastraat on your left.

Map 5.4 – A few more steps will bring you to number 37, also on your left.

Fire Station

This was at one time The Hague's fire station – you can imagine the fire engines pouring through the gateway to save someone's home. It was in use until 1969.

On either side of the main archway you can see some carved symbols representing the firemen, a helmet, a ladder, and an axe.

Right at the top is the usual Stork.

Map 5.5 – Backtrack to Juffrouw Idastraat on your right-hand side.

Walk along Juffrouw Idastraat to number 7 on your left.

This is the entrance to the Jacobus & Augustinus Church

Jacobus & Augustinus Church

Officially Catholicism was outlawed in Protestant Holland in the seventeenth century, however the Dutch are a very easy going nation, and as long as they didn't see it, they ignored it. So secret chapels appeared in towns all over Holland, but only a few survived – this is one of them.

It was built in the early eighteenth century and it was deliberately made to look like a normal house from the outside, but if it's open it's worth popping through that door.

You walk along a little corridor before entering a bona fide church. It also happens to be quite beautiful. Of course those columns are not actually made of marble; they were made out of wood but cunningly made to look like marble. They give interesting tours on Sundays.

Upstairs there is another chapel, the Attic Church – which is still in use on Wednesdays.

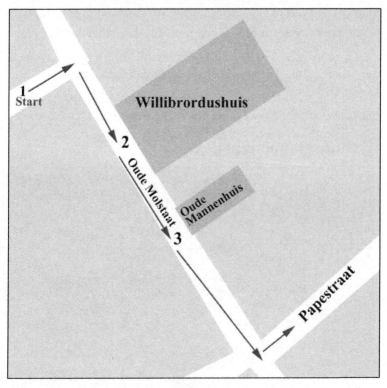

Map 6

Map 6.1 - When you leave the church, turn left to reach the junction with Oude Molstraat.

Turn right along Oude Molstraat. At number 35 on the left you will find the door to the Willibrordushuis Chapel shop.

Willibrordushuis Chapel Shop

The chapel was unusually once home to both monks and nuns, although only monks are found here now as the nuns left in 1988.

If you go through the door you will find yourself in the order's little shop. Ask if you can visit the chapel which is upstairs. It is very beautiful with lovely stained glass windows. If the brothers are at prayer you must be very quiet and discrete.

On your way out have a look around the shop – you could buy some of the Trappist beer brewed by the monks!

Map 6.2 - Just a little further along, you will reach the brick built Old Man's Home at number 25 on the left.

Oude Mannenhuis

It has the founder's coat of arms above the door. It was in use as a retirement home until 1980.

Buildings such as these sprung up all over Holland for poor men over sixty, to give them a clean place to sleep and food. Holland did this because the consensus was that old men couldn't look after themselves, unlike old women. That left the older almshouses for the elderly women who were able to look after themselves.

Of course institutions such as this always have their own rules, such as mandatory attendance of church. But I guess that was a small price to pay for free care and lodgings.

Sadly, like a lot of buildings in The Hague, the doors are only open on Heritage Days. This building was renovated in 2012. The main rooms are wallpapered in landscape paintings, and one of them conceals a hidden door. During the restoration they discovered a sixteenth century cellar.

Map 6.3 - Continue down Oude Molstraat to the junction with Papestraat where you turn left.

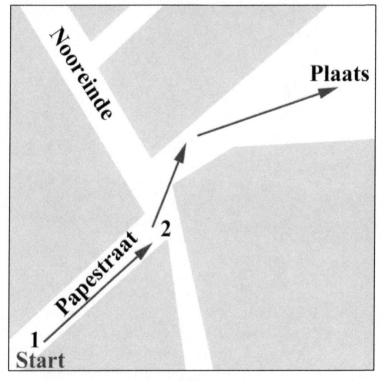

Map 7

Map 7.1 - Now it's just a brisk walk along Papestraat to reach a T-junction.

143

Map 7.2 - Turn left and take a few steps along Nooreinde. Then turn right to return to Plaats.

You have now reached the end of this walk.

Walk 4 - The Peace Palace

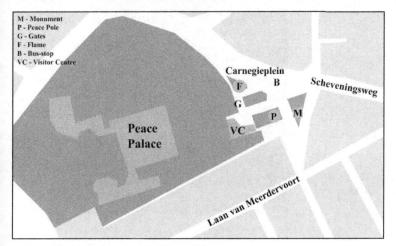

Walk 4 Overview

The Peace Palace is a bit out of the old town centre. The easiest way to reach it is to catch tram number 1 heading towards Scheveningen.

Get off at Vredespaleis, and from there you can see the Palace gates.

There is a landscaped area in front of gates which have some interesting items to have a look at.

Carnegieplien

Face the Palace and on your left is the columned Resistance Monument.

There are also some convenient benches - especially useful if you are waiting for your time-slot to visit the Peace Palace.

Resistance Momument

The monument was placed here at the end of the twentieth century after a campaign by the surviving members of the Dutch resistance, and a ceremony takes place here on Remembrance Day each year in May.

The sculptor was Appie Drielsma – a Jewish survivor of World War II. Its four small pillars symbolise the four groups in Dutch society at the time of World War II: neutral, Roman Catholic, Protestant and Jewish.

Now take a few steps towards the main gates of the Palace.

Peace Pole

On your left you will see a Peace Pole which was placed here in 2013.

There are Peace Poles in various places all over the world; all bearing the same message "May Peace Prevail on Earth" in various languages. Here, in front of the Peace Palace, seems a very good location.

The Gates

The ornate entrance gates are made of wrought iron, and were given by Germany just before WWI. Look at the middle panels from both sides – they depict Amicitia, Pax, Justitia and Concordia, or Friendship, Peace, Justice and Concord – a bit ironic coming just before World War I!

To the right of the gates is the Peace Flame.

Peace Flame

In 1999 the World Peace Flame Foundation lit a flame in Wales. The flame inside this pillar was taken from the flame in Wales and has burned since 2002.

You might not notice at first but its stands in a little rock garden. The 197 rocks come from the 197 nations who have signed the world peace agreement.

The visitor centre stands to the left of the gates.

Visitor Centre

If you have arrived without tickets you can enquire here what your options are.

Peace Palace

At the very end of the nineteenth century, the nations of the world were invited by Tsar Nicholas II of Russia to a peace conference and 26 countries responded – perhaps driven by a desperate hope that they could avoid war, as Europe was arming itself at a terrifying rate.

The Tsar chose The Hague as the location, mainly because his cousin Wilhelmina was queen there and it was easy access from most countries. Once assembled the delegates decided a permanent conference centre was needed, and since they were in The Hague already it was decided to put it there.

To finance the building they approached the millionaire Andrew Carnegie who was willing to stump up the cash – on condition that the building also included a legal library. The library eventually became the International Library of Law. Building started in 1907 and the palace opened in 1913 - but sadly failed to stop WWI breaking out one year later so perhaps the Powers didn't do enough talking.

After WWI the League of Nations was assembled and its International Court of Justice was placed in the Peace Palace. However, once again war broke out – still not enough talking.

During WWII the International Court of Justice shifted to Switzerland for safety, but returned to The Hague when peace descended. After the horrors of two world wars, the League of Nations transformed into the United Nations. It's mostly based in New York, except for The International Court of Justice which is still here in the Peace Palace. The court is frequently asked to arbitrate when countries have disputes.

Touring the Palace and Gardens

Various countries showed their enthusiasm for peace by giving gifts or valuable building materials when the Palace was constructed, and if you do the tour you will see many of them.

You will see a bronze statue "The Spectre of War" given by Chile. It is quite frightening - it depicts War looming over the dying.

The clock tower holds a Swiss clock. It bears an inscription in German which translates as "My bells want to ring in the peace"

The Exterior

As you approach the palace you will see a beautiful fountain decorated with polar bears which was given by Denmark – It seems an odd gift as there are no polar bears in Denmark, however Denmark ruled Greenland at the time so perhaps that is the connection. The bears and other animals were made by a porcelain factory and are very delicate – in winter they cover the fountain up completely. It fell apart in the seventies and was restored in 2007

In front of the palace is the Eternal Flame.

You enter the Palace by climbing a flight of steps made of granite, given by Norway. You then enter by the iron and bronze art nouveau style doors given by Belgium.

The Interior

The Entrance Hall

The hall is quite overwhelming and runs the length of the palace. The sumptuous pillars which you see on both sides were given by Italy. They are made of Carrera marble, which was Michelangelo's absolute favourite. The glowing golden lamps with crystal covers came from Austria. At either end stand the Great Hall of Justice and the Small Hall of Justice.

The grand staircase was given by The Hague itself, and on its landing it hosts The Statue of Justice from the USA. It differs from the traditional Justice as she has no blindfold and has discarded her sword and scales.

You will also see the seven stained-glass windows from the Netherlands, with Irene, the goddess of Peace, standing with a golden sun behind her. Also at the top of the stairs is Christ the Redeemer of the Andes, a replica of the statue which stands between Argentina and Chile. It was made from cannons of both countries. They came close to war but it was averted by King Edward VII of the United Kingdom who was known as The Peacekeeper. It's been pointed out that putting a Christian symbol in an International multi-cultural setting such as the Peace Palace is inappropriate – but he is still there.

The beautiful floor is also Italian marble and is inscribed with:

"Sol justitiae illustra nos",

"The light of justice shines upon us."

The Great Hall of Justice

The stained glass windows were given by the UK. France gave a painting, La Paix et la Justice, which shows Irene, the goddess of Peace, between two battling armies.

The Small Hall of justice

The room's main decoration is a tapestry "The Glorification of Peace" which was a gift from France. It is left unfinished because its artist was killed at the Somme in WWI.

This room had to have its floor re-enforced to hold the jasper and golden vase given by Russia. It weighs in at 1,200 kilos. On it you can see the symbol of the Romanov family - a two-headed eagle   Find the statue of Tsar Nicholas who started the whole Peace Palace off. He and his family perished in Russia's revolution.

Japanese Room

This beautiful room is decorated using precious wood from Brazil and six Japanese tapestries. The tapestries were crafted by over 48,000 weavers from silk, and took five years to complete. The enormous carpet is one of the largest in Europe and was presented by Turkey. The large vases are from China. More controversial are the tusks from Thailand which probably couldn't be accepted nowadays.

Peaceful men

As you go round you will see many busts of men of peace. Most you won't recognise but there are some everyone knows about, Nelson Mandela, Mahatma Ghandi, and King Edward VII.

The Library

The library which Carnegie insisted on was first housed in the Palace, but is now in its own building connected by a footbridge. It holds some rare books by local boy Hugo de Groot

Hugo de Groot

Hugo de Groot is better known as Grotius who wrote Mare Liberum (The Free Sea) in 1609. It eventually formed the basis of Maritime Law.

He wrote it try to justify the seizing of a Portuguese ship laden with treasure by the Dutch East India Company. His argument was that the sea is international territory, as opposed to the Portuguese claim that they owned the trade routes to the East Indies. The statement that the ship seizure was lawful as it broke up the Portuguese monopoly sounds very dubious! The various maritime countries argued back and forth until they came to the conclusion that the sea was owned as far as a cannon could be fired from land – which evolved into the three mile limit. Nowadays that has been extended to a twelve mile limit – after all we have bigger cannons now.

The Gardens

These were designed by an English gardener and are a delight in summer when in bloom. The water running through it is from The Hague Creek which you might have read about earlier.

If you have time you can find the cornerstone of the Peace Palace on the NE corner. It is inscribed with a thank-you to Carnegie for financing the project.

Once you have finished exploring the Palace, return to Carnegie Square and catch tram 1 back into town.

Did you enjoy these walks?

I do hope you found these walks both fun and interesting, and I would love feedback. If you have any comments, either good or bad, please review this book

Other Strolling Around Books to try:

- Strolling Around Bilbao
- Strolling Around Arles
- Strolling Around Bruges
- Strolling Around Ghent
- Strolling Around Verona
- Strolling Around Palma
- Strolling Around Ljubljana
- Strolling Around Berlin
- Strolling Around Jerez
- Strolling Around Porto
- Strolling Around Lucca
- Strolling Around Amsterdam
- Strolling Around Madrid
- Strolling Around Lisbon
- Strolling Around Sienna
- Strolling Around Delft
- Strolling Around Florence
- Strolling Around Toledo
- Strolling Around Bath
- Strolling Around Antwerp
- Strolling Around Pisa

Printed in Great Britain
by Amazon

47734093R00086